No Such Thing as a Bad Dog

Why your dog exhibits unwanted behaviour and how to fix it

Fenella Nicholas

Copyright © 2022 Fenella Nicholas

The moral right of the author has been asserted.

Apart from any fair dealing for the purposes of research or private study, or criticism or review, as permitted under the Copyright, Designs and Patents Act 1988, this publication may only be reproduced, stored or transmitted, in any form or by any means, with the prior permission in writing of the publishers, or in the case of reprographic reproduction in accordance with the terms of licences issued by the Copyright Licensing Agency. Enquiries concerning reproduction outside those terms should be sent to the publishers.

Matador
Unit E2 Airfield Business Park,
Harrison Road, Market Harborough,
Leicestershire. LE16 7UL
Tel: 0116 2792299
Email: books@troubador.co.uk
Web: www.troubador.co.uk/matador
Twitter: @matadorbooks

ISBN 978 1803131 504

British Library Cataloguing in Publication Data.
A catalogue record for this book is available from the British Library.

Printed and bound in Great Britain by 4edge Limited
Typeset in 11pt Minion Pro by Troubador Publishing Ltd, Leicester, UK

Matador is an imprint of Troubador Publishing Ltd

No Such Thing as a Bad Dog

For Ben, Mia and Lucas: masters of living life
to the full and taking each day as it comes.
Reminding me daily how to be more dog.

Contents

Introduction ix

PART ONE 1
How to Stop Things Going Wrong in the First Place

Chapter 1	Choosing the Right Dog	3
Chapter 2	Boundaries	9
Chapter 3	Rules	12
Chapter 4	Training	17
Chapter 5	Introductions	20

PART TWO 29
Common Problems and How to Fix Them

Chapter 6	Jumping Up	40
Chapter 7	Lead Pulling and Door Barging	47
Chapter 8	Recall	58
Chapter 9	Prey Drive and Chasing	65
Chapter 10	Obsessions	70
Chapter 11	Separation Anxiety	75

Chapter 12	Destructiveness	85
Chapter 13	Fear	90
Chapter 14	Aggression	102
Chapter 15	Resource Guarding	117
Chapter 16	Copraphagia (poo eating)	130
Chapter 17	Inappropriate Toileting	133
Chapter 18	Excessive Barking	138
Chapter 19	Quirky Behaviour	145

PART THREE 153
Keeping on the Right Path

Chapter 20	To Neuter or Not to Neuter	155
Chapter 21	Diet	167
Chapter 22	Mental Stimulation	176
Chapter 23	The Walk	182
Chapter 24	Impulse Control	187
Chapter 25	Communication	193
Afterword		205
Notes		207

Introduction

All dogs are born perfect. Left to follow their natural instincts in the wild, they live in harmony with each other and their surroundings. It is only since dogs' domestication that problems have arisen. Dogs in the wild have no problems. No quirky behaviours or obsessions, no chewing up the den or endless barking. At worst, there may be a tussle over food, but as soon as the pack leader steps in, the problem is resolved. Even street dogs are happy, left to their own devices. The intervention of humans has created a myriad of problems. By taking dogs into our homes, we are asking them to behave unnaturally – to be left on their own without their pack, to be handed food on a plate without having to work for it, to have no job or purpose, to receive only affection without discipline. Essentially, they are adaptable creatures, in the hands of a knowledgeable owner, but too often a lack of leadership and understanding is where things start to go awry.

I am contacted when things have gone wrong. I specialise in behaviour modification and training. You could call me a dog whisperer, a behaviourist, a canine psychologist, but I am really just an unglamorous creator of normal. I am passionate about dog welfare and helping owners get the best out of their canine friends. I would find it near impossible to function without a dog in my life. The rewards of a loving bond are immeasurable, and I hope to be able to create the same joy for as many dog owners out there as possible. But it's not always easy. Don't assume that the second you bring your new dog home you have your fairly-tale life laid out before you. Often it's exactly the opposite. Panic at the enormity of the responsibility you have taken on, guilt for having to leave your dog to conduct your own life, fear of what might happen to the dog if you can't fulfil its needs. This is all normal, and means that you CARE. You are willing to do something differently for the good of your dog, and I commend that. Reading this book is the first step to your road to recovery.

I trained under the umbrella of Cesar Millan, the renowned 'Dog Whisperer' in the United States, whose ethos is to connect with a dog by being more doglike ourselves; to speak their language, rather than expecting them to speak ours.

I'm uncomfortable with book titles such as 'From Puppy to Perfect', which suggests it is only our involvement which makes dogs perfect. In my job, alas, it's more of 'From Perfect to Pitiful'. It is precisely our involvement which turns faultless young dogs into complications. They become fearful dogs, destructive dogs, bored dogs, possessive dogs, hyperactive dogs, dominant dogs; but never bad dogs. We can't call them bad dogs when they are merely acting the way we have shaped them, intentionally or not.

When things go wrong, it can mean a multitude of things: the dog is too aggressive, too shy, too noisy, too anxious, too rumbunctious. Strangely, I have never been called up and had an owner moan about their dog... "Alfie is a total nightmare! I struggle to walk him, I have no control of him and I don't feel I have any bond with him. You are my last resort before I give him away." Instead, I'm pleased to say, all owners seem besotted with their hounds. Most conversations begin, "Alfie is so sweet. He's such a loving dog, and really wants to please. He's perfect in every way. Except there's just this one thing..." As I unravel the story, it often becomes apparent that there is considerably more than one thing which is a problem. Or quite often that one small thing can be quite a significant thing, such as growling at the toddler in the house. Alarm bells. A serious issue which must be nipped in the bud immediately. A growl can lead to a bite if unheeded or unchecked. No matter what the issue is, so far, I have never been told afterwards that my journey was fruitless. I'm happy to say there is always some improvement after my visit. And contrary to popular belief, no dog is too old to change, and no problem is too ingrained to improve upon.

No dog is badly behaved on purpose. Dogs live in the moment, not fretting about the future, or worrying about the past. They do not rationalise. They don't soil the house in protest of you being absent, and they don't go out looking for a target to attack. All their actions are responses to how they feel at any one given moment. This is why I have to come at a problem from the dog's perspective. If your dog knows what the rules are and breaks those rules, there will no doubt be a very good reason for it. For example, a client of mine has a Labrador who is not allowed on his mistress's bed. For years he has honoured this rule until one day he kept trying to not just get on the bed, but *in* the bed. She would scold him and shoo him away. It was only recently that she discovered, on a visit to the vet for some vomiting, that he had Addison's disease. One of the symptoms is very cold feet. Poor thing was simply trying to warm himself up under the duvet, to combat the cold, and keep his health intact. So, you see he is in fact a clever dog, not a bad dog.

There is a reason why dogs do every problematic thing they do, and you can bet we are behind all of them. They may attack an oncoming dog, if you have tensed the lead, signalling you are unsure; they may chew up their bed because they are bored and you haven't taken them out or interacted with them enough; they may eat poo because you are feeding them a poor diet, or because they always get your attention when they do; they may obsess over inanimate objects because they have no outlet for their energy. It may be unwanted behaviour, but it's not intentionally *bad* behaviour. If anything, it's 'bad owner', not 'bad dog'.

I don't mean to alienate you, kind reader – just the fact that you are reading this book points to your concern and dedication to put things right. My aim is to make you aware that our actions are key. They have created a behaviour, but new different actions can 'uncreate' it. **We change, our dog changes.**

I'm usually contacted by an owner to discuss one particular problem. Let's say it's that the dog is barking at everything that walks past the door, and that he stands in the garden and just barks, waking up the neighbours. (Incidentally, it's normally upsetting the neighbours that prompts them to call, not the fact that the dog is obviously stressed!) I walk in and we have a chat about when the problem started, what they've tried so far (which obviously isn't working), what rules are in place, how much exercise the dog gets etc, and I soon discover that he pulls dreadfully on the lead, has high prey drive and only comes back when he is ready, and howls when the owners leave the house. Suddenly, but not surprisingly, I am faced with a host of other problems too – separation anxiety, poor recall and general bad manners. Everything is connected. I will teach proper lead walking and how to leave the house. "But we brought you here to sort out the barking" they might say. "The lead pulling doesn't bother us". So, I have to explain that it is precisely the lack of rules that is contributing to the dog not respecting our command when we ask him to stop barking. He is being the leader – literally leading his owner out the house and down the street, so of course he feels in control. When he stops, his owner stops, when he speeds up, his owner speeds up. The dog is the pack leader, so why should he take orders when told to be quiet from the pack follower?

I try to address all the issues in one session, as all cogs of the wheel need to be sorted for the changes to work. But often one session is not enough, and I leave the owners with foundations to work on before we move on to the next step. With the barking dog, we set up some basic house rules and boundaries first. I returned on another visit to address the issue of separation anxiety, and I returned again to work on recall. When the owner changes their behaviour, the dog just slips into line.

I have divided this manual into three parts. I would urge you to resist the temptation to jump straight to the chapter which deals with your dog's particular problem. Reason being, like I said above, many problems are interlinked, and you can't always fix a behaviour by addressing just the one issue. It needs a more all-rounded approach. I hope to have provided useful tips in every chapter, without repeating myself in each one. Therefore, to give yourselves enough ammo to tackle a singular problem, you would be wise to glance over every chapter. After all, prevention (and nipping unwanted behaviour in the bud) is better than cure.

Sidenote: Please do not be offended if I refer to all dogs in the masculine. It is simpler and avoids confusion. There is greater sensitivity these days towards gender, and I would hate anyone to take offence.

PART ONE

How to Stop Things Going Wrong in the First Place

I'm guessing you are reading this book because you have a dog with an issue. It may be too late to 'stop things going wrong in the first place', as things have already gone wrong. But don't let this put you off reading Part 1. All dogs, no matter how far down the line they are, need boundaries, rules, socialisation and training, so read on.

But before we start, I would like to address an issue that may be obvious to some, but surprisingly not so to others: your dog is an animal. Not a human, not a baby. He has animal wants and needs. It is a common habit to anthropomorphise your dog, but it is not doing him any favours. Dogs do not need a fluffy pillow, a personalised bowl, clothing, hand cooked food. It is not healthy for them to be washed every other day, or to be carried around like an infant. They are not a fashion item or a prop for your ego. Dogs need to sniff each other's bums, need to dig and to hunt, need to be walked and exercised, need to meet other dogs, need mental stimulation, need to be led and guided. By taking them into our homes we have a duty of care to them, and we must be respectful of their dog needs, not our own needs.

Dogs should not be made to behave like humans. It is wholly unnatural for them to do so. Nor do they think like humans. To believe that they experience jealousy, guilt or anger, and that these emotions drive their behaviour, does our canine companions a great injustice. If anything, we should endeavour to become more dog-like, rather than forcing them to become more human-like. My behaviourist business is called 'Be More Dog' for this very reason. Understand your dog from his point of view, and you will soon realise that there really is no such thing as a naughty dog.

CHAPTER 1
Choosing the Right Dog

I have never heard a client of mine say, "Well we took a long time choosing the right dog that would fit in with our lifestyle and match our energy." This is ultimately why they end up calling me – because they didn't do that. Far more common is, "We didn't choose the dog, the dog chose us", or "We felt so sorry for him we just had to take him home".

These are both dangerous situations where emotions have clouded the vision. Either we feel so flattered that a dog has trotted over to us, or we start a relationship based on sympathy. Neither are healthy.

If it's a specific breed you are after, make sure you do your homework first. Don't be surprised when the dog starts showing behaviours he was bred for. If you want a terrier, don't get annoyed when he starts digging up your garden. If you want a sight hound, don't get frustrated when he runs off at full pelt into the distance after anything that moves. If you want a lap dog, don't expect him to be able to be left on his own for hours on end. That said, you may presume that nature determines a dog's traits and personality. But this is only the tip of the iceberg. All experiences the dog has in his life will be moulding and shaping him. Everything we do, or fail to do for him, will have direct consequences. If he growls at your husband but not you, if he chews up the house, if he barks all day long, if he stares obsessively at shadows, you can bet we have created it all. So, I would argue that nature plays its part, but nurture is everything.

The first golden rule is never to buy a puppy from a puppy farm, or one that is less than 8 weeks old. Most people would not knowingly do this, but can be conned into it. Bitches on puppy farms are used as baby producing machines for financial gain only, with little or no concern for the dog's welfare. Conditions are often terrible and the dogs lead a stressful life. This stress is passed on to the pups. A dog that is taken from its mother before 8 weeks of age is missing out on discipline and valuable lessons she will teach him. Good breeding is EVERYTHING. Poor breeding is where things go wrong, before you have even brought your puppy home. Poor breeding will affect your puppy for the rest of its life. Do your research. Don't rush into it.

Always insist on visiting the breeder and seeing the puppies with their mother. Does mum look healthy? Does she look old? You don't want to be tricked into buying from a disreputable breeder using mum for litter after litter. Do you warm to the mother, or is she nervous, barky, fearful of strangers, overprotective of her pups? All these characteristics may well be passed down onto her offspring. Find out about the sire (father of the litter). There may be more than one for a single litter of puppies. What is dad's temperament like? If you can't meet him in person, ask to see a photo. I would be suspicious of anyone unable to show you one. Ask to speak to the sire's owners. What are the pups being fed? Ask to see the ingredients on the packet. There should be a high protein content (over 60%) and no cheap fillers like rice, grain or soya. Is the litter being raised in a home, surrounded by household sounds? This will make it easier when you bring your puppy home to your own home. Does the breeder have children? This may seem like a strange question, but if you have children of your own at home, you will want the puppy to already be used to the sounds of kids crying, shouting, laughing and generally banging around. You will also want the pup to have had some experience of being handled by more inexpert hands. On the flip side, beware of a breeder with small children who might be allowed to over handle the puppies. This can cause stress and lead to your puppy developing a fear of being picked up or a fear of kids. If this fear goes unnoticed by you, the excited owner of your new puppy, it can lead to nipping, in the puppy's attempt to keep hands away. Now you could be dealing with a fear reactive dog for the next fifteen years. So it's worth asking all the right questions and doing your homework from the start.

If the breeder is not asking you as many questions as you are asking them, then walk away. Their primary care should be the welfare of their puppies' future homes. Your first visit should feel like an interview. You can expect to be asked, "Who will look after the dog when you go back to work?", "Do you have a garden?", "Do you have any other pets or children?"

When choosing a puppy from a litter, you should consider its temperament, and not just go for the one with a patch shaped like a heart, or the one that walks over to you first. If you let the dog choose you, it will probably be the first of many decisions the dog will make instead of you, and set you up for a whole bunch of trouble. There are various tests a qualified behaviourist can perform on a litter of puppies to determine which are suitable for family homes, and which would be more suited to more experienced owners or working jobs such as guarding or police dog work. An ideal pup should be interested in you, and not go off on its own. He should not mind being handled (no wriggling or stiffening), and should not protest when he is gently pushed away from a bowl of food.

Be careful when picking the runt of the litter. In the wild the mum might ignore this one and even let it die. After all, the survival of the pack depends on all members being healthy. Pity is a very human emotion, and it can get in the way of raising a balanced dog. We might then spoil the runt more, or impose fewer rules, which creates many of the behaviour problems listed in Part 2. Similarly, if choosing a dog from a shelter, you might go for the most helpless looking one, cowering in the corner, or the one which got run over and has a limp. I'm not saying it's not an honourable thing to do, to take these damaged dogs into your home, just start off without getting your emotions involved. Treat them like any other normal dog, and then you will be helping them in the best way possible.

The clever way to choose a dog is to take your time, and draw up a list of what you want in a dog. Find one that matches your energy and your lifestyle. It's no good if the dog you want bounds around non-stop, if you are a more sedentary individual; or if the one you want is shy and unsure of himself, and you are the gregarious, garrulous type who enjoys lots of home parties. We owe it to our dogs to give them the best home possible for their needs. You may find that fate has an uncanny way of giving us the dogs we need, rather than the dogs we want. I used to rush around a lot, trying to juggle so many jobs to the detriment of my health, but my old Labrador has taught me to be patient and made me slow down. I literally have to walk her at a snail's pace. Our energies matched when she was younger, and it has evolved into something beautiful. What is your dog teaching you?

I get many enquiries from people looking for help training their puppies. Regretfully I put the phone down without being able to help most of them. (Well, I am able, but I choose to keep my skills for the more damaged dogs). I refer the puppy training to a colleague of mine, and tell the owners that I hope not to be seeing them further down the line, or it will mean the puppy training hasn't gone to plan.

When I say puppy, I generally mean a dog below the age of around 6 months. (Although puppyhood stretches on for a full year.) I'll make exceptions and see a puppy if there is a problem developing that needs addressing straight away. For example, I took on a terrier that was growling and biting the whole family at only 4 months old. This could not be left to fester and escalate.

In this section I will not give you a full-on puppy training low down – you will no doubt have a separate book for this – but rather guide you through the basics to get things started in the right direction. If you have rescued a dog, or come by one later in its life, the information in this chapter is still relevant, as it should be applied throughout the dog's life.

The majority of dogs I see as a behaviourist are small breeds. It's not that small dogs per se have more problems. It's more that owners don't discipline small dogs, as they would feel the need to do with a large dog. They don't lay down rules and boundaries from the start perhaps because they presume that even when fully grown, a small dog will still be small. They will still be controllable physically. For example, you may think it won't matter if a Jack Russell jumps up at people because they are too small to inflict any damage. I think the cockapoo is the breed that comes to my door the most. Whether this is because they are particularly cute as puppies – they look like teddy bears – and the owners just cannot bear to tell them off, or whether it's because they're just so popular, every other household has one, I can't tell. More likely it's because this fashionable crossbreed is misunderstood. People assume they are getting a perfect mid-size breed, 'hypoallergenic' non-shedding, playful, intelligent dog. What they are actually signing up for is a lifetime of a dog with no 'off' button, who needs masses of mental and physical stimulation on a daily basis, just to stop it chewing up the house or constantly pawing you for attention. Both poodle and cocker spaniel are working breeds and without being put to work, they suffer.

Whatever the breed, your puppy will be cute and small. We have a natural predisposition to baby these traits, and believe that an outpouring of love will create the perfect pet. But love alone, with the absence of any rules when the pup is very young, can lead to problems when they are older. If your pup is allowed to jump up on you and mouth you when he is small, how will he know that he is no longer allowed to do this once the bite starts to hurt, or once he has knocked over a child? Best to set up some rules from the get go, and stick to them.

CHAPTER 2
Boundaries

Firstly, set some boundaries. Just like children, dogs need rules and boundaries in order to be able to relax and know what's expected of them. The *first boundary* is your personal space. It's very disrespectful for a young dog to go bounding into another dog's personal space, without pausing or sniffing first. If he tried this on with an older dog, he might be met with a growl, by means of trying to teach him some manners. Similarly, the pup should not be allowed to go jumping up on you. A mother might correct her offspring with her mouth, so I try and mimic the mum's mouth by putting my hand into a claw shape and prodding the pup in the chest. The strength behind the prod will depend on the response from the pup. Always use the minimum force required. I accompany the prod with a vocal 'uhuh'. This prod tells the pup to back off and slow down. An alternative method is simply to walk away when your pup jumps on you. All household members must give the puppy the same message, so as not to confuse him. If one person strokes the pup when he jumps up, and another prods him, he won't know whether to expect a reward or a reprimand. Consistency is key.

The *second boundary* is rooms in the house. I have met many an owner who admits proudly that the dog can go anywhere it likes. They believe that this is being kind to the dog, giving it all the space it could possibly need. However, this is where problems can arise, because of a lack of respect for boundaries and limits. Introduce your pup or newcomer to one room of the house at a time, over some weeks. Do not give him too much independence too soon. There should always be a room that the dog is not allowed in, even if it's just the bathroom. With a pup, you could use a staircase at first to cordon off rooms, but I will show you in chapter 24 how to get him to stay out of a room with no physical barrier, just by practising impulse control. A dog behind a closed door is just itching to get to the other side of it. They can work themselves up into a frenzy scratching at the door and barking, and they learn nothing. But if the door is open and they wait respectfully behind the threshold, they are learning self-control. This is the psychological exercise. My dogs are not allowed upstairs or in the basement, and they respect this. The only time my Romanian rescue tried to creep down into the basement was during a particularly noisy firework display. Not naughty – just survival mode kicking in.

The *third boundary* is your furniture. If your dog has the run of the house, your sofa, your bed, he may start to believe he owns the house. We don't want him becoming more powerful than us. It creates a multitude of problems, including resource guarding, possessiveness, separation anxiety and aggression.

I'm not a complete ogre though. I realise that quality bonding time is spent with your hound cuddling on the sofa in front of the TV, or bedding down together. Go ahead and

How to Stop Things Going Wrong in the First Place

do this, sure, but make sure your dog is *invited* up by you first. If he jumps up uninvited, just push his rear gently and say "Off". Repeat *every* time he jumps up again. It may be that your dog has his own armchair or spot on the sofa. That's fine, but make sure he knows which ones are off limits.

You may be interested to know that within a pack of wild dogs, the pack leader claims the best sleeping spot and does not share it with the rest of the pack. So, if you allow your dog to sleep in your bed, you are sending the message to him that you are just another pack member, not the leader. But hey, if your dog is perfectly behaved, knock yourself out. After all, it's only natural for dogs to want to snuggle up with the rest of their pack. I just wouldn't recommend starting this ritual with a young pup just to get him to sleep without howling, and just because it makes you feel good. You may be creating a rod for your own back.

CHAPTER 3
Rules

How do you think your kids would turn out growing up without any rules? Unruly, spoilt, confused, tired? It's the same for dogs. Some people mistakenly believe that the kindest thing they can do for their dog is to let him do whatever he wants, go wherever he wants, feed when he wants. Fortunately for me these people keep me in business. Not so fortunate for the dogs though. When a dog has no direction, he is left to make up his own mind about decisions, which can be stressful for him. This can lead to mistrust and a lack of bonding and an unsettled dog with behavioural issues.

What the rules are going to be, depends on person to person, home to home. But there should be some. Rules actually help your dog relax, knowing that someone has control of everything. Your dog can then take a step back from their guarding, or their fear, or their hyperactivity, or whatever it is. It may sound strange, but it's so much kinder to bring up a dog on rules than letting him have free rein and free run of the place.

When I have my initial consultation with a client, one of the first questions I ask is, "What rules are there in place?".

For the most part I am met with silence, or laughter. This makes my job pretty easy. Introduce some rules, and watch the magic happen.

Here are few to get you set up:

- Follow the boundaries as set out in the previous chapter. This means no jumping up, no access to every single room in the house, and keeping some furniture off limits.
- Don't feed at table. Not just because if you do, it encourages you to be pestered every time you sit down to eat, but more importantly because it will tell the dog you are on his level, not the leader. In the wild the pack leader would not share his food with the rest of the pack, and they respect that. Sharing food from your plate is telling your dog you are just one of the pack. This will make things harder for you when you are expecting him to obey your commands. Why should he do as you say if you are just a playmate and not a figure of respect?
- Work for food. Do not leave food down all day. All dogs should be incentivised to eat. This gives them a purpose. At the very least a dog should sit and wait, and give you eye contact whilst his food bowl is placed on the floor. Preferably he should have a long walk before any food, or perform a mental task, or some agility. Dogs in the wild hunt if they are the parents, or wait for the parents to return if they are the young. Both

can be considered 'work'. Life becomes very dull if a food bowl is permanently on offer, like an all day buffet. Dogs who have shown no interest in their dried food, have come to life and eaten it when they have had to work for it. For example, if you make a game out of throwing the food or hiding it. I have had my Romanian rescue for 8 months and have always fed him one handful at a time. He has to do something for every handful: sit, stay, roll over, spin, shut the door, jump up, play dead, sit pretty, heel, leg weave, retrieve etc. That's roughly 480 meals to date. Around 4,800 handfuls, and he's done something for every one of those handfuls. He knows a LOT of tricks! And it's been invaluable for bonding.

- No excitement at meal time. A dog that barks and jumps up, or demands his food, is not giving you the space and respect he should. If you let him do this, the message you are giving him is that you are just another pack member, you're not the boss. This may have a knock-on effect with his other behaviour – pulling you down the street, jumping all over you, not able to calm down. Wait for calm before giving the food. If you have multiple dogs, feed the calmest first. It's also better for their digestion and health if they are in a calm state before they eat.

- Give eye contact. Eye contact with your dog reminds him to trust you; to look at you for guidance or permission before everything he does. A dog who gives good eyes is usually a keen

How to Stop Things Going Wrong in the First Place

learner and has a great bond with his owner. If your dog avoids your eyes when you say his name, try making a kissy noise. If he looks up, the second your eyes meet, mark it with a 'yes' (or a click if you are clicker training), and then reward with a treat. If you are still struggling to meet his gaze, try this: at feeding time, put down an empty bowl. Likelihood is, he will look up at you as if to say, "Huh, where's the food?" The second you meet eyes say "Yes" and put a tiny handful of food in his bowl. He will finish it pretty quickly and then look up as if to say, "Is that it?" Say "Yes" again for this second meeting of eyes, and put another handful into the bowl. Continue in this way for the entire meal.

- I use eye contact to reset a dog who has poor recall, or who is reactive. It just brings him back to you mentally, reminds him you are there, and stops him from getting too stuck in to his environment. You don't want to become invisible to him. Some rescue dogs are so traumatised that it may be a while before they look you in the eye. After all, dog-to-dog eye contact can be threatening. I never look a dog in the eye when I first meet him in his home as this can be perceived as challenging him.
- No pulling on the lead. I will go into this in detail in chapter 7.
- Wait. Learning a bit of impulse control is very important to help your dog think for himself before making decisions. He should be able to

wait on a slack lead, or at your side, before going through the door. He should wait for permission before going to his food bowl once it is on the floor. He should be able to wait at the bottom of the stairs while you go up. He should be able to wait without protesting or whining as you chat to friends in the park, or sit and have a coffee. (More on impulse control in chapter 24.)

- Good recall. Coming back to you the first time you call. (See chapter 8.)
- Drop. It's useful to have a release cue, in case he picks up something when out and about that he shouldn't be eating. He should drop a toy/ball on cue too. This will prevent any resource guarding and aggression over possessions. It is unwise to play tug of war with your dog (unless he is placid) – especially if you let him win.

CHAPTER 4
Training

A friend of mine with her relatively new 11 week old puppy asked me when she should start training. "About three weeks ago", was my reply. As soon as your 8-week-old puppy walks in the door he is ready and capable of learning simple commands such as sit, lie down, come, stay. Most people believe that housebreaking is the only training necessary at this stage. But start all training from day one, including the rules and boundaries, and you will be giving your puppy a sense of focus and enthusiasm essential to a well-mannered pet.

Never punish or scold. This can create a fearful or aggressive dog. Use positive reinforcement to enforce the behaviour you want. But do not ignore unwanted behaviour. By ignoring, you are allowing. Use the minimum negative reinforcement necessary. This could be in the form of a stern tone of voice (not yelling), or a touch correction.

Crate training is another useful tool. Dogs are denning animals, and like snug spots to eat and sleep. The crate should represent relaxation and not punishment. It's a place the dog can go for time out when he needs to rest. Position it away from the hustle and bustle of family life, (but close enough he doesn't feel totally excluded,) especially if you have a noisy household. When things get too much for him, it's good for him to know he can go somewhere for peace and quiet where he won't be disturbed. If you have young children, dissuade them from going in the crate with him, or bothering him while he is in there. The crate also teaches him to be separate from you, in the kindest of ways. (More on separation training in chapter 11.) Feed in the crate, chill in the crate, nap in the crate. The crate should be just big enough for the dog to stand up and turn around in, and should grow with your dog. (Most have a moveable wall.) Any bigger and they may soil in one end and sleep in the other. Dogs do not like to soil their sleeping areas, so a smaller crate teaches them to hold their bladders and aids toilet training. A pup can usually hold his bladder for one hour per his age in months. Therefore a three month old pup can hold his bladder for 3 hours during the day and a little longer at night. That said, I have had clients report that their 10 week old pups remarkably slept through the night in their crate with no accidents.

If it's a puppy you have brought home, take him to puppy training classes. Not only will you learn loads, but it will be great for his socialisation with other dogs and people, and he'll love it. Sadly, most people stop the classes after a few sessions because they have mastered the basics, but the alternative for the pup is often sitting at home doing nothing. So as long as your wallet can stretch that far, continue with the classes. When he's outgrown puppyhood, maybe move on to flyball classes or sled pulling, or lure coursing or agility – depending on what's suited to his breed and what naturally turns him on.

Throughout the course of his life, it's wonderful to be able to continue with training of some kind, no matter the age or breed. Your dog will be eager to learn, and it will be a fulfilling time for both dog and owner. There is always a new trick to master, an obstacle course to tackle or a puzzle to solve. (See chapter 22: Mental Stimulation.) If you have a working breed, give him the natural outlet he needs for the job he was bred for. For example, if you have a herding breed such as a collie or a heeler you could try treibball (herding a large exercise ball into a goal), hide and seek, fetch with various objects (ball, frizbee, dumbbell etc) or flyball. If you have a hunting breed such as a beagle or a dachshund you could lay a scent trail or bury a favourite toy in the garden for them to dig up.

While it is good to consider the job a dog was bred for, and look for suitable outlets for game playing, it's also useful to consider his senses. Does he like physical touch (like a Labrador)? Does he have acute hearing (like a Lhasa apso or terrier)? Is his nose permanently on the ground following a scent (like a bloodhound)? Or does he rely on his sight more than his nose or ears, (like a lurcher)? Perhaps you have an oversensitive dog who does not like being touched or who is afraid of loud noises, like an ex-street dog. Or perhaps you have a dog who is lacking in some senses – he may be going deaf or blind. Take all of this into consideration when finding him appropriate games and training. Any training at all is brain training, which dogs need on a daily basis to lead a fulfilling and enriched life.

It's never too late to train a dog or teach him new behaviour. You *can* teach an old dog new tricks. **There are no untrainable dogs. Just untrained humans.**

CHAPTER 5
Introductions

While your puppy is still young, introduce him to as many different sights and sounds as you can. We don't want him to be phased by anything later in his life. Take him in the car, on a train, past a noisy building site, introduce him to livestock, give him a bath and a blow dry. Walk him past old ladies with walking sticks, men in hats, children screaming. Take him to the vet for no reason other than to get used to that environment and have someone else touch him and prod him. I wouldn't encourage 'pass the puppy' which some trainers recommend in socialisation classes. I understand that they are trying to get the pup used to being handled by different people, but in reality it can be stressful for the pup, and he may even develop a mistrust of strangers. You want the bond to be between you and your puppy alone.

Do not rush to get the above list of introductions done in a few days or your puppy may get completely overwhelmed. Overexposure can be as damaging as underexposure. For example, an overhandled pup can lead to fear of being handled as an adult. A pup who is led up to every single dog it passes in an effort to 'socialise' it may lead to a fixation of other dogs. Teach your pup to walk on by or to watch other dogs. Just sitting on your doorstep watching the world go by can be one of the best places to start socialisation. Take everything very slowly.

Do socialise your new pup responsibly with other dogs. A dog who has not learnt how to interact with other dogs can grow up to become dog-aggressive, or dog-fearful and they can be difficult to train. But be careful; inappropriate socialisation can do as much harm as lack of socialisation. If your puppy practises the wrong kind of play with another dog – and by this I mean being bullying or getting overstimulated – and if there is no intervention from the owner, then this can lead to dog-on-dog aggression later. So always ask yourself, "What is my puppy practising now?" If yours is the puppy being bullied, and you do not step in, he may also learn to use aggression as a defence mechanism.

Make sure all the new meetings and experiences are pleasurable for your puppy and reward him for not reacting. Watch and learn from a distance what he likes and what he doesn't like. If he shows any discomfort then remove him. You can try again at a safe distance next time until he feels more comfortable. Remember, your future relationship with your new best friend will be based on trust in these early days and months. Work as a team. If he's trying to tell you he's had enough, or moves away, or comes to hide between your legs, respect that and help him. Interestingly, tiny amounts of stress are actually good for a very young puppy as they help to build his stress immunity, but by age 8-11 weeks old it's the fear imprint stage of development, and important that all experiences are positive.

If you have adopted a dog (ie a rescue) you may not know what environment he has come from, and what he is familiar or unfamiliar with. Introduce new sights and sounds sympathetically. When you first bring him home, do not force your friends on him. Let him settle in for at least a week. He may not even be ready to go outside for a week. Take things very slowly and be respectful of his space. Do not keep going up to him and trying to engage him. Let him come to you when he is ready. You could walk past his bed and drop a treat, and then walk away. You want to leave him sniffing after you with an outstretched head, not cowering away from you. Always try and create forward motion, and leave him curious and wanting more.

Do not rush to take your rehomed dog with you everywhere. Start with the back garden if you have one, or the area directly outside your front door. Over the first few weeks just walk around the block, or in an area very close to your house. Slowly progress to include a local park. Make sure he is happy and familiar with this park before taking him to a different park. Gradually increase his world over the following weeks, not days, to include a coffee shop, public transport or your friend's house. As with my advice for a new puppy, listen to him – if he looks uncomfortable with any of the new places, remove him.

When my 3-year-old ex-street dog came to live with us, he was scared of everything: sudden movements, loud noises, going through doorways, traffic, the hoover, unfamiliar objects, unfamiliar people etc. When he first came home, I made sure that the children were away at school for a full week before coming home. He had enough to contend with even with just me and my husband at home. New smells, new sounds, new surroundings. Many people believe that the moment you 'rescue' a dog and give him his 'forever home', everything will be perfect. Sadly it's often the start of a very stressful time for the dog. The changes can be overwhelming and exhausting, and many rescues shut down when they arrive in their new homes. They can also do lot of sleeping as they adjust to and process their new surroundings. Be patient and be predictable. Set a regular timetable for meals and pee breaks to create a reassuring pattern. You probably won't see your new dog's true character for months.

After some months, once Rocky had settled in, I gradually introduced him to the things that had previously triggered him. Slowly, and one at a time. Rather than remove all the things he was scared of, which I see many of my clients do, I made each thing a positive experience. This is called counter-conditioning. For example, he had a huge fear of my guitar at first. To him it was a massive object that I waved around which emitted an awful sound (when I was playing it anyway). So step one was just leaving it lying around, making it a common sight and smell. Then I left pieces of food on it, and walked away. His curiosity and appetite eventually got the better of him and he approached closer and closer every day until eventually he ate the treat from the body of the guitar. We progressed over the following months to him playing it! I'm not kidding – I taught him to strum on the strings. He loves to perform for his favourite piece of cooked chicken. So you see, some introductions can take many months.

Older dogs will teach younger dogs how to behave. They may growl at a boisterous adolescent who has run up and jumped on them, instead of approaching with a polite gesture such as a low head and using their nose. People are quick to judge the growler as the bad guy, when in actual fact he may be the good guy trying to instil good manners. Similarly, a mother will correct her young, either with a hard stare or by growling or picking them up in her mouth. It's vital that puppies are not taken from their mother before 8 weeks of age, or they are missing out on this crucial learning period.

Our dogs also learn from watching their owners. For example, don't pick your dog up just because you are afraid of that mean-looking big, black dog approaching. Stand between him and the big dog to show him you will protect him, but picking him up is teaching him that there is something to be afraid of, and you may unwittingly be nurturing a distrust of all big, black dogs. There is a male couple I see regularly in my local park who constantly carry their fluffy Shiba Inu puppy around in their arms. On the rare occasions they put her down, I would watch them scoop her up again every time another dog approached. Horrified, I went up to them, "Oh dear, has your dog got something wrong with its legs?" I knew perfectly well it didn't, but wanted to be a bit thought-provoking, and didn't want to go barging in criticising. "No, she's just very scared", they replied. I stated my profession and very gently explained that they were teaching her to be afraid. "Have you worked with Shiba Inus before?" one of them replied, almost accusingly, as if all the problems were breed related. I intimated it was less about breed and more about them – I gave them my business card, and not surprisingly, never heard from them. I still see them from time to time. The dog is now fully grown, and they have progressed to carrying it around in a backpack, as it's too heavy for their arms. Occasionally they put the dog down and for the most part it just sits there quivering. It makes me so cross. They have made the dog like that. The dog was perfect until they came along and put their fears on her. That poor dog's world is now very small indeed, and fuelled with nerves, which will in turn put a strain on its health – the very health they were trying to protect.

I often see similar behaviour with the owners of Chihuahuas, and so called 'handbag' dogs. These dogs can be treated like toys or babies due to their small size, and they are very often carried around. This only teaches the dog that the ground must be a very unsafe place to be. Fear aggression to keep 'threats' away may then develop.

If your dog does experience a genuinely frightening occurrence, it's important *not* to try and console him. By doing so you will be nurturing that state of mind. It's a very human emotion to do this, to stroke and use sweet talk, but the dog is actually being rewarded by the stroking and is learning that to get your praise and approval he should be afraid. Use distraction instead. Lead him away from the frightening thing/place. Act relaxed, and stay close to be a quiet reassurance.

Part of the rehabilitation training I do in cases such as this, is exposing the dog to its triggers or fears in a very controlled way. I use my own very balanced unreactive dog as a gentle buffer. If my dog does not react to what the other dog fears, then the other dog gets the message that maybe that 'thing' is not so bad after all. I show the other dog that nothing bad happens. On the contrary, something positive will happen, by way of a treat or toy, whichever the dog is more responsive to. If we take away everything the dog reacts to, we are taking away part of the rich tapestry of life from him. Instead teach him not to react, and to trust.

If you have a reactive dog, (or a rescue, as mentioned earlier,) be careful about introductions. You don't want to put them through any unnecessary stress if they find some other dogs or humans hard to cope with. If you have a nervous dog, it's your job to protect him from his fears. Keep visitors to the house away from him until he is ready to go and sniff them. (See chapter 13: Fear.) Dog-to-dog introductions should always be done on a slack lead, or they may sense tension from you and feel you need protecting. Basically, a tight lead can start a fight. (See chapter 14 on Aggression.) Dogs meeting each other off lead usually sort themselves out, communicating with their body language, but there may be times when an owner needs to step in. For instance, if play becomes too excitable, or if your dog becomes aggressive. Of course, it's better to step in before the aggression has even occurred. Intervention from the owner is one of the key actions that can stop things going wrong in the first place. This is why it's so important to swot up a bit on dog body language. You'll then be able to tell if your dog is uncomfortable around another. Sometimes it's kinder to cross the road to avoid an oncoming troublemaker, than to make your dog walk past and have to defend himself by lunging. After all, if he's on the lead, how can he possibly show he's not a threat by taking a wide arc around the other. Walking head-on in a straight line toward another dog can be quite confrontational.

If your dog is one who is quicky aroused and goes from playing to growling and nipping at his playmate, please don't say what I hear so often – "He's only playing". You need to call him away, get him to focus on you and calm down before allowing him back into the foray. You are 'invisible' to your dog if you allow him to get too stuck into his surroundings. He will be making his own decisions. Often the wrong ones.

The correct way for a human to say hello to a dog is to *ignore* it. **No touch. No talk. No eye contact.** He may not be comfortable with you approaching him, bending over him, putting your hand on his head. It's all very intrusive. Allow the dog to come and sniff you. (You may want to crouch down, side on, to show you are no threat.) Once he has done this, you have gained his trust somewhat, and can venture to put a hand on his shoulder. Not on his head, which can be threatening. Do not pursue a dog who is trying to avoid you – ie turning his gaze away, turning his head away, walking away. Trust takes time to build. Be respectful and go at the dog's speed, not yours. In severe cases this could mean weeks or months. It took a year before Rocky would allow my head to rest touching his.

PART TWO

Common Problems and How to Fix Them

I'm not actually keen on the word 'fix', as it suggests our dogs are broken, but it is a word we all understand. Something is not as we'd like, and we want to change it. We may have been the unwitting creator of the problem, or we may have inherited a dog with problems. Either way, we would all like a quick fix. Some *will* be quick overnight fixes, some will take longer, much longer – months or years. Some issues are so ingrained they can never be eradicated, just managed. It depends on the severity of the problem and the dedication of the owner. If you do see a behavioural problem creeping in, don't delay in seeking help from a behaviourist. The longer you put up with it, the harder it will be to cure.

Many owners out there have sought the help of a behaviourist, given it their best effort, and remain at their wits end because the problem is still there after months or even years of training. They have vowed never to give up on their dog, so they continue being stressed, and their dog continues to be stressed. Sometimes the best course of action for both parties is rehoming the dog. There is no shame in it. It's not 'giving up', it's providing your dog with what is best for him.

I know a lady who adopted a young dog from Romania. He had been living in a shelter in the UK for a year, to recover his health, as he was in such a bad way when they found him. The shelter was in the countryside and not overcrowded with too many dogs. There was a huge field the dogs could run free in and a group of friendly volunteers who were all familiar faces to the dogs, and occasionally walked them further afield. Happy that the dogs were well cared for, the lady decided to adopt. She ensured that the new dog was accustomed to her and her other dog before taking him home. She was an experienced handler, and settled him in slowly, at his speed, knowing that a new home in the heart of a busy town would be a huge challenge for him.

It was not to be an easy ride, and nor had she expected one. She was just happy to have 'rescued' an animal that may otherwise have been put down. The dog had many fears, and aggression issues towards men. She hired a specialist in rehoming street dogs to more fully understand his needs. She worked daily training him and trying to make him feel secure. Slowly a trusting bond began to form. Then the pandemic hit. Her and her family moved to their house in the countryside, not far from the shelter, to sit it out. The dog thrived. No traffic, no doorbell, no partying teenagers, no joggers, no strangers, no sirens. Just long walks, sniffing out pheasants and running free, surrounded by the same 4 trusted family members every day. No surprises. It was a joy to see him so relaxed and happy.

At the end of lockdown, the family returned to the city. Old behaviours resurfaced. New behaviours emerged. Bonfire night came along and seemed to put a nail in the coffin. Fireworks were let off every night for two weeks continuously. Like a war zone. As soon as daylight began to fade, the dog would creep down into the basement boiler room and make himself very small, curled up in a little ball, immobile until a new day dawned. This is the most pitiful state for a dog to be in, and is called 'learned helplessness'. He has learnt that his only option is to shut down completely and pretend not to be there at all.

He became more reactive on walks when off lead, and more reactive inside the home. The lady's stress levels soared. This, in turn, led to a vicious circle of more stress from the dog, which created further stress in the owner. The dog was not happy. Seeing him so unhappy made the lady unhappy, though she loved him dearly.

Having seen her dog so at ease in the countryside, she knew what had to be done for the wellbeing of the dog. She could not bear for him to live out the rest of his life confronted by his triggers and fears on a daily basis. She contacted the owner of the shelter. It had been a year since they had spoken. She asked if the shelter could find a more suitable home for him, in the countryside, single owner, no kids. She would write a report of all the dog's nuances and needs, and hold on to the dog until a new home was found. This of course could take months.

The owner of the shelter, without hesitation, offered the dog an immediate home with her and her pack. They lived on the shelter site, so it would be familiar ground, familiar faces. The lady's shoulders dropped about a foot when she heard this and she began to cry tears of joy and relief. The dog was going home.

I inserted this story having finished writing the book, unsure of whether to include it or not. But in the end I felt it was important for you to know that sometimes things are just not meant to be. The lady in this story was me. I thank Rocky for all the happiness he brought, and for the wealth of knowledge he brought to my door.

Just occasionally, rehoming is not an option. Rehabilitation has not worked, and the only recourse is to have your dog put down. I have never recommended this course of action, and I hope I will never have to. I can't imagine the pain and suffering this choice gives to owners who can see no other way forward. Behavioural reasons why a dog or puppy may have to be euthanised include terrible breeding that makes the dog so unwell that he can't function in the world; resource guarding instilled at birth by poor breeders; aggression which poses a threat to the public; a level of fear that cannot be reduced and renders the dog unable to operate.

But most problems can be solved or improved upon. Whatever the problem is – and there's usually more than one – it takes consistency, patience and dedication from the owners to get results. If you correct your dog from jumping up on you one day, but can't be bothered the next, your dog will be confused, you won't get the results you want, and you will be calling me again to say the game plan hasn't worked. EVERYBODY in the household, including visitors to the house, and the dog walker, all have to be giving the same message to the dog, 100% of the time. All the humans are the pack leaders.

Your dog, however, may only see one person in the house as the leader, but it's my aim to have him respecting and obeying everyone in the house. I often hear one spouse say to the other, "Well he never does that with me". It's abundantly clear then that it's not the dog at fault, if he is capable of behaving perfectly with one person. It's then my job to work on the weaker human, the one the dog respects less. I'm really not training the dog at all.

Dogs are constantly reading our energy. They will follow **calm assertive** energy. They do not respond to shouting or being made to feel afraid, or to weak energy – someone who doesn't really mean what they say, or doesn't think it's going to work. A pack of dogs in the wild would pick out the calmest, mentally strongest dog to be their leader. After all, their survival depends on that leader making the right decisions and guiding them to food, shelter, water and out of harm's way. The rest of the pack can then relax, knowing their every need is taken care of and that the pack leader is looking out for them. We humans have to step into those shoes and be the calm assertive leader, if we want to gain our dog's trust. Some trainers talk about the importance of the owner being the "alpha dog" and about dominating. I'm not keen on these terms, or methods. They suggest bullying your dog into submission rather than creating a trusting bond that makes your dog want to follow you. Other trainers disagree with the term 'pack leader', and believe that love and friendship alone will see you through. In my experience, dogs feel secure knowing that someone else is in control. How better to do this than to mimic what occurs in a pack of dogs? Speak a language the dogs understand. My company is called 'Be More Dog' with good reason.

I believe in using a mixture of positive and negative reinforcement to get your dog to understand what is expected of him. Many behaviourists baulk at the idea of using negative reinforcement to train a dog. If you are one of these, let me tell you a little story to see if I can get you to view things differently. I am quoting here a piece by Peggy and Allan Funnell, members of Goldsithney Dog Training Club:

"I would like to tell you about a trainer I know. People should make their own judgement about her methods...

This trainer's speciality is training puppies, although she can handle adult dogs too. She adores puppies, but has definite ideas about training them. She does play with them, but not when training. She uses no praise that I have ever seen, and no rewards. Her rules are simple but must be strictly adhered to. She is always the boss. If a pup does not do as it is bid, punishment is swift and to the point and the pup understands exactly what she means.

Most of the time she grabs the pup by the nose or the scruff of the neck. If the pup is really bad, she forces it to the ground, making it stay there until it submits properly. She totally approves of grovelling and of dogs crawling on their bellies on occasions. She also uses the above methods with adults when necessary. Older dogs who have known her since puppyhood roll over in complete submission on meeting her...I suppose it could look like fear but to me they seem to adore her almost above any other being.

Common Problems and How to Fix Them

No doubt you are wondering if I like her, and if so, how could I condone anyone who trains in such a way... By now some of you will be furious about this person, and would like to give her a piece of your mind. I don't think she will take much notice, because she knows, like most trainers, that her methods are effective.

I will tell you her name.
It is Whisper.

She is a collie dog who has had several litters. I have watched her train her babies and pups which have been brought into the house. Without exception every pup she has reared and trained loves her dearly, even though some are now into middle age, and all respect her."

Although I do not use Whisper's forceful methods, I do understand that some negative reinforcement may be necessary in order to get a message across. If we come at a problem from a dog's point of view – this is where the psychology comes in – we are able to communicate our feelings better, and you will have a better connection with your dog.

Bitches reprimand their offspring to maintain order. They use physical and vocal corrections to discipline their young, so it's an interchange dogs respect. They get speedy results, and are effective in creating total trust. Would you bring your child up on praise alone? You would create a monster if you did. Children, just like dogs, need to be told what to do, as well as what *not* to do. By not disagreeing with an unwanted behaviour, you are actually *allowing* it. Distraction onto another task will not get the message to sink in like a simple, "You're not to do that please".

Let it be clear that by negative reinforcement I do not mean punishment. Punishment does not work and can in fact make the situation worse. Contrary to popular belief, dogs do not know when they have done wrong. That 'guilty' look on their face when you come home to a shredded sofa, that's appeasement. They are merely reacting to your body language and tone of voice, and predicting you are about to do something to hurt them. And guess what – they shredded the sofa not out of naughtiness but because they were bored and frustrated, because *someone* is not giving them the exercise they require. If you were to punish a dog who did this, you would make the dog anxious and fearful and perhaps he might even become aggressive, to protect himself from the anticipated beating. What's worse still is that the dog would have no clue what he was being beaten for. Result – zero trust, zero bond. They cannot associate a past event with a present one.

What I mean by negative reinforcement is letting the dog know with a correction that what he just did is unwanted. The correction must be administered at the exact time the unwanted behaviour is happening. It could simply be a vocal correction. I find "Uhuh" works particularly well as it does not betray any anger (as 'no' can), and sounds like no other word. Another correction is a short sharp tug AND RELEASE on a slip lead which has been positioned in the *correct* way, up behind the ears, so it does not put pressure on the dog's windpipe. It's a bit like getting a tap on the shoulder.

Just enough pressure is exerted to snap the brain out of its current way of thinking, and back onto you. Thirdly, the touch correction is one I use frequently. This is how a mother would correct her own pups. She 'bites' with her open mouth onto the pup's neck or rear. I try and mimic the mother's mouth and teeth by making a claw of my first 2 fingers and thumb, and use this to prod (no pain) a dog's chest or rear. Lastly, I use body language and eye contact to correct and assert myself. I stand tall, chin up, perhaps hands on hips if I really want to get a message across, and I stare directly at the dog. This gives him a very clear message I mean business. Again, this is a language dogs understand, as a head (and tail) held high, and direct eye contact is a confident challenge.

Whichever correction is used, it's vital that the MINIMUM FORCE NECESSARY for your particular dog to respond, is administered. A skittish cockapoo will need a very light touch and regular tone of voice; a feisty terrier may need a stronger touch and a sterner voice, bull breeds stronger still; a fearful street dog would need no touch at all, and a soft voice, possibly crouching down to his level sideways on, with no eye contact, to show him you are no threat.

More often than not, after a session with a client, and having prodded the dog on its rear, tweaked the lead, told it to get off the sofa, used my body to block it, and had some assertive words, the dog wants to follow me out the door! They are just so relieved that finally here is someone to take control. They can relax.

Positive reinforcement comes in the form of a reward for behaviour you approve of. It could be a treat, a toy, vocal praise, softly stroking. It's really important to reward the good behaviour, otherwise the dog will learn that he only gets your attention when he does something you disapprove of. When he is sitting calmly on his bed behaving himself, that's a great time to go up and gently stroke him, or give him a rub or a massage. Always reward the calm.

Having said that, it's important to note that the use of 'good boy/girl' can in fact be read as a release cue by the dog, and send him back into misbehaving mode. For example, if you have asked a dog to stay on his bed, and he is staying, choosing that moment to say "Good boy" for staying, will usually have him leaping off his bed towards you. Sometimes it's better to say nothing so as to maintain the dog's concentration, and save your praise for the end of the entire exercise.

When I meet up with a client and their dog for the first time, I summon up positive energy beforehand. I enter knowing wholeheartedly that I will make a difference, that the dog will respond to me. I am a firm believer in the power of positive thinking. I try and persuade my clients to do the same; to envisage the result they want to achieve and to think, 'This is going to work'. If you believe it's going to work, it usually does, because you are giving off the correct signals to the dog, who picks up on this. Sadly, some clients would rather be proved right than enter into the programme as I suggest. "I'm not sure that will work" and "See I told you", are common phrases from the doubters. In these cases, changes sometimes don't happen at first, and I have to get them into the right frame of mind. My main aim during a session is to show them what the dog is capable of. If I can get the dog to stop barking or to come back to me the first time I call, or to stop his obsession, or to get him to ignore another dog he would usually lunge at, then I have shown that the dog can do it, and we're half way there. The hard part can be getting the owner to repeat what I have done, and to follow through with consistent practice. Sometimes the great results tail off after a few weeks, and I get a call saying it's not working any more. In these instances, I know it's not the dog, and I have to concentrate on the human.

Below I have set out some of the problems I get called up about most. Although I offer a way to deal with each problem, it is worth noting that every dog is different. With a different breed and temperament, and without seeing that dog in person, hearing their history, meeting the owners and seeing the house set-up, it is impossible to tailor the solutions to each individual dog. What I do offer, I hope, is an understanding of the kind of change required by the human. You will have to temper the solutions to match your dog.

What I will tell you off the bat is that there isn't much which can't be fixed through exercise and discipline. Affection is very low down on a dog's needs. Affection is *our* need. Affection is often the *cause* and not the cure of some behaviour problems. If you remember nothing else in this book, remember the words of the Dog Whisperer, Cesar Millan, that dogs need:

> "EXERCISE, DISCIPLINE, AFFECTION –
> IN THAT ORDER"

CHAPTER 6
Jumping Up

This is a habit that pretty much all dogs go through. They are taught it. As puppies they jump on us and we show them our approval by stroking them and saying hello in a super friendly and excitable way. This encourages further jumps: after all, we've just told them it's what we want. Then we go out to the park and the same dog jumps on the nearest person he sees to please them and he is met with shrieks of horror from his owner, as his feet are muddy and his victim's trousers are pale cream fresh pressed linen. How confused he is now! "Do they like me doing it or don't they?", he must be thinking.

Sometimes young dogs will jump up to grab a treat or a toy from us. If we are not ready for the toy to be grabbed, we will lift it up higher, out of the pup's reach, but actually encouraging the pup to jump up and grab it in a fun game of chase. When you first get your new dog, reward a sit as often as possible to encourage 'four on the floor'. Reward with a treat delivered below his chin. This will stop him from jumping up to get it and stop him thinking all treats come from above. Play games on the floor with toys at low level, so he doesn't get conditioned into jumping up for them.

The best idea is to impose a 'no jumping' rule from the off. The reason is twofold. The first is obvious – to save you and your friends' legs from dirt and scratches, and to prevent someone being pushed over. Even a small dog can put a toddler off balance. The second is a matter of respect. Dogs would not tolerate being jumped on in their world. It's normally just the young pups that do it in play. Allowing them to jump on us signals that we are just their playmate, not their leader. If we are not their leader, why should they obey us? Therefore, regardless of the size of your dog, your personal space is the first of many boundaries he should learn to respect.

Firstly, I'll tell you what doesn't work: yelling "Down" repeatedly, and flapping your arms about. This is just fanning the flames of excitement. You are engaging with your dog and giving him the attention he was after. Nor does turning your back work. You are just giving your dog a bigger target to jump on, without the ability to push him down. You're essentially saying, "Here you go mate, jump on this!" Another method I have heard people recommend is holding the dog's two front paws when he jumps up, and not letting go. I haven't tried this myself, but I imagine you would spend much of the time with very dirty hands, and it might even be giving the message, "I want you up here and I'm going to keep you up here".

What I have found to be effective is simply to walk into your dog as he jumps on you. Dogs do not like being put off balance, especially if it's sideways. If your dog is consistently put off balance when he jumps up on a family member, and does not get the attention he was after, he will soon stop trying. It should be done with no eye contact, no talk. The key to success is to get every household member to do the same, *every* time. If one weak link bends down to stroke him after jumping up, you will be back to square one, and he will have learnt just to be more persistent next time.

If you are seated when he jumps up, you could always stand up, so he 'falls' off you, or without engaging eye contact or talking to him, push him down. Repeat as often as he jumps up. Though if you are using the correct calm assertive energy, he should get the message and not try again.

The hardest bit of training a dog not to jump up is controlling other people's reactions to it. The last thing you want is for someone to stroke your dog (praising him) when he's jumped on them, after days or weeks of your hard counter conditioning work. When visitors come to your home you must simply ask them to ignore the dog until he is calm. If he jumps on them, you must step in and push him off. You can then use your body as a blocker and stand between the dog and his target. If your dog jumps up on people when out and about, my advice would be to have him on a long line until he has learnt what the rules are. You can then call him to you before he gets to them (with a tug if he ignores), or if you are too late and the deed is already done, then at least you can pull him away. It's important that the pull is a short sharp tug and release, to snap the brain out of its current mode of thinking, rather than a long steady pull, which isn't really teaching him anything. He must do the moving away himself, if he is to get the message.

My sister has the most delightful spaniel, Pepper, who in truth I would love to steal for myself, as she is very responsive, affectionate and keen to learn. My sister and her family have trained her well, but the jumping up is one area they yoyo on. Pepper spends three days a week at my parents' house when my sister goes to work. Rather like doting grandparents spoiling a child and lapsing on the rules, they positively encourage the jumping up and reward her with sweet words and caresses when she does. I have often witnessed the exasperated looks from my sister, at family gatherings, when Pepper has jumped on my father's lap at meal time, and is rewarded with a kiss. But what can she do? They are doing her a huge dog-sitting favour, and have chosen to do it their way. Without consistency, the dog just ain't gonna get it.

I often say 'A calm dog is a happy dog'. An excited dog is in an elevated energy state – the brain is in overdrive and it is a challenge to get their concentration. If a dog is to learn, he should be calm. We are in control of all our dog's emotions. We can gee him up, or calm him down. When you come home and your dog is at the door jumping all over you in excitement, and you feed that excitement by greeting him enthusiastically and rubbing him all over, you are effectively teaching him that coming and going is a big deal, and he is right to get all worked up about it. (Not a good idea for dogs with separation anxiety.) He will most likely learn that jumping up is wanted and encouraged by you. It's a very human need, not a dog need, to be greeted by an over excited dog. It makes us feel special. But if you seriously want to stop the jumping up behaviour, you have to do the hardest, most counter-intuitive thing an owner has to do: completely ignore the dog. He will soon calm down in the absence of any encouragement. (This is also good practice for dogs who pee themselves with excitement.) When he is calm, go and lavish all the affection you like on him. Calmly. This way you are saying, "I approve of the calm". Because you are nurturing the calm state of mind, you will be offered more of it, as your dog learns and wants to please. And in turn the jumping up will cease, and your dog will be happier.

My dogs do not jump over me or my guests, but they do gently wag their tails and come and have a sniff. They are rewarded with caresses. However, if you are happy with your dogs jumping up, and *they have no other behavioural problems*, then that is your decision. But do bear in mind that not allowing the jumping up is teaching them to respect you and your personal space. Being jumped on would not be tolerated in the dog world, and I try and teach my clients to 'be more dog' and behave the way dogs themselves understand.

There are always exceptions to the jumping up rule. If you have a young puppy or a fearful dog, you may find that when they become overwhelmed, for example in a dog park, they will jump up at your legs. They are asking you for help. Do not ignore this or push them down. If you push them away every time they seek your help, they will soon change tack, and maybe next time they will run away and out of the park, or protect themselves through aggression. The correct response in this case would be to crouch down, giving them a protective cover, or to walk them away. Try to resist the temptation of picking them up, as this will be reinforcing that the ground is an unsafe place to be.

When I first adopted my Romanian rescue, he was very mistrusting and shy and fearful. After about 2 months, he greeted me in the morning by placing his two front paws delicately on my middle. This was a bit of a breakthrough as he had never sought out my attention before. I did not discourage his actions. In fact, I did completely the opposite, and stroked him gently as he rested on me, telling him this was behaviour I was pleased with. He does so now every morning in a very calm frame of mind, and it is our most bonded time of every day, and I relish it. It means he is feeling confident and that his trust in me and his environment is building. Remember, the 'rules' are not hard and fast, but fluid, depending on your particular dog and his state of mind. Context plays a huge part, as in all behaviours. Is your dog doing 'hard' jumping up, the sort that knocks you off balance and certainly gets the desired effect of grabbing your attention, or is he doing 'soft' jumping up, more as a polite greeting, where he keeps most of his weight on his back feet? It's only the former that needs addressing.

When a person comes to your door, it is often one of the highlights of your dog's day. The door can represent new exciting sights, smells and interaction at a time when he has nothing else to do. It's no surprise then that many dogs rush to the door to investigate, and this heightened state of being elicits barking and jumping up. A well-balanced dog will give the visitor space on entering and then walk up and sniff them. The sniff is like a handshake and tells them a myriad of information. To obtain this balanced welcome I suggest the following: when the doorbell goes, your dog will most likely alert you there is someone there. All good. You then have to ask him to stand down – his job as sentinel is done – you can take it from here. Get between him and the door and walk towards him so that he backs up a good couple of metres. Tell him to stay. Do not go to the door until he has stopped barking and has calmed down. Take as long as you need. Practise with a willing and patient participant the other side of the door. Maintain eye contact as you back away to open the door. If he steps forward take a step towards him, so he backs up again. You can also give a vocal "Uhuh", but otherwise zip it. Use the power of silence and your body language. You are having a conversation, the dog way. Repeat this dance as often as you need until he stays put. Open the door slowly, still maintaining eye contact with your dog. He'll most likely rush forward if you turn your back on him or greet your guest with high pitched tones. Once your guest is in the door, your dog can come and sniff hello. Since he is in a calm state of mind, he will be far less likely to jump on them. Tell your guest only to greet the dog if the dog stays with four paws on the ground.

CHAPTER 7
Lead Pulling and Door Barging

Do not underestimate the power of the walk on a lead. You and your dog are physically connected, and it's a chance to be wholly in control of him. Off lead, he is making his own decisions. If you get it right, he should be barely perceptible, mirroring your step.

Pulling on the lead is a pretty mediocre nuisance on the scale of other dog problems, especially if your dog is small. But allowing it, just because your arm is not being pulled out of its socket, could be giving the wrong message. You are effectively saying it's fine for him to lead you, and it's fine for him to not listen to you. Correct lead walking is linked to a host of other issues, which is why whatever problem the dog has, I always ask to see lead walking first. If the owner can command the walk, he can command elsewhere.

If you have a dog which barges out of the door ahead of you and pulls you down the street, he is leading the walk from the start. He will be making his own decisions, quite often the wrong ones, and this in turn can be stressful for him. The walk begins inside the house, as soon as you reach for the lead or put your coat on, or pick up your keys. Since your dog does nothing all day except watch you, he will know these cues instantly. He will get up in anticipation of going out. There is no need to excite him further with a high pitched "Walkies" or your equivalent. If he exits the house when his brain is in a state of excitement, you will be feeding that excitement, and whatever 'problem' he is manifesting, (be it pulling on the lead, barking at other dogs or people, chasing cats or joggers or bikes) will be exacerbated.

On my walks with clients, I ask them to leave the house as they normally would. A typical scenario would be: the owner calls the dog, who starts a game of catch-me-if-you-can. Having chased the dog around the house, the owner tussles for a while trying to get a harness on. He then wraps the lead a couple of times around his hand and opens the door. The dog shoots out the door dragging the owner behind him. The dog, then on a long or retractable lead, zigzags wheresoe'er he pleases. When the dog stops to sniff or pee, the owner stops. When the dog is ready to move on, the owner follows. It's only when I ask, "Who do you think is leading the walk?", that the penny drops.

It's my job to turn that around. The owner should be leading the dog. It's a way of saying, "Trust me. You can relax". We then go back to the house and leave all over again. My way. Firstly, the dog should come to me. If he doesn't come when called, or tries to change it into a game, I might waft the smell of something delicious under his nose to engage his attention, then I walk away. He must remain calm or I go and sit back down again. I make a loop out of the slip lead and put it in front of him to sniff. I don't want him to be scared of any new equipment. I put a treat the other side of the loop, and he puts his own head through it. I gently pull the end of the lead so it tightens around his neck. All calm, no sudden movements, no words.

I pull the lead up behind the dog's ears, above his windpipe, and lock it snugly into place. If I give a pull on the lead, I don't want the dog to choke, hence the positioning is key. Higher up on the neck is also the weaker part, so making it harder for them to pull with. Some behaviourists oppose the use of slip leads and put them in the same category as choke chains and prong collars. This is because they don't know how to use them correctly and humanely. Of course, any constant pulling on a noose-like lead around a dog's windpipe would cause discomfort. I never let the dog pull constantly. A short sharp tug AND RELEASE on the lead, signals to the dog they are doing something unwanted. It snaps the brain out of its current way of thinking. At all other times the lead should be SLACK. The lead correction is usually enough to have the dog understanding what is wanted within a few hundred yards. As long as it is administered with the correct calm, assertive energy. I often accompany the lead correction with a vocal "Tshh" or "Uhuh". Eventually, sometimes even by the end of the walk, the dog will respond to just the vocal correction and not need the lead correction any more.

I understand why people turn to a harness for a dog which pulls. They are trying to stop all that pressure on the dog's neck. But the reality is that the harness allows the dog to use his full body weight to pull *more*. What do you put on a husky to pull a sleigh? Exactly. I'm also not a fan of any contraption that goes around the dog's legs, as they usually inhibit free natural movement or dig in. The flexi-lead is another tool which I discourage. Although I can see the practicalities of it, it gives constant pulling pressure around the dog's neck. I want the dog to only feel pressure when it has done something unwanted by its owner.

Now the dog is calmly on a lead, we approach the front door. I open it a crack. If the dog rushes forward, I close it again. The dog generally backs up, and I open the door again. We can continue this 'conversation' until the dog understands that only by backing up and waiting does the door open. This can take some time, so for a quicker result you can open the door wide but just stand there. When the dog rushes forward, give a short sharp tug on the lead and then release it so it becomes slack. The dog learns nothing if you are holding him back on a tight lead. He must do the waiting himself. This is the psychological exercise. He must be able to stand in front of an open door without assuming he can go through it. I don't need him to sit, just to hold himself back. When he is not pulling, I walk forward and he walks with me at my side. Up to this point I have not said a word.

The exact same scenario should be repeated when you come home, and at every doorway you encounter on your walk: the gate to the park, the door to the pub, your friend's front door.

If travelling in a car, your dog or dogs should show the same respect and restraint when getting out. You should be able to open the door without them rushing out. They need to look at you first for permission. Block their exit with your body. Only when are they calm, should they be allowed out, otherwise they will shoot out like catapults and this excitement will have them jumping up on the first person they see, or if they have aggression issues, biting the first person/dog they see.

It may be that you have a dog who has an aversion to going outside or through doorways. In this case, the lead pulling will be from behind and not in front. A bad experience in the past may have triggered this. Although dogs live in the moment, they have very good memories. If a door has closed on a dog's body causing pain, or if the dog has experienced frightening noises outside, for example, he will associate going out as a possible repetition of those experiences and seek to avoid them. It's our job then to reset his neural pathways and show him, with the use of repetition, that nothing bad will happen. In these cases, the dog needs some gentle, yet assertive encouragement, to get up and move. Depending on the dog's nature, I might put the slip lead on and matter-of-factly say, "Let's go", whilst giving a gentle tug and release on the lead, and slowly moving forward. If you do it with the right energy, and if your dog trusts you to keep him safe (because you have put rules in place), then he will follow. It is important to imagine the end goal in your head. Say to yourself, "I have no doubt he will follow me out the door" and he most likely will. If you think it'll never work, it most likely won't.

Do not drag your dog along the pavement on his bum. He is not learning anything except to resist more. The lead correction snaps his brain out of its current thought, and sends a message to his legs to move. Now he's learning, and moving forward on his own, without having to be dragged. That is the psychological exercise.

Once you have managed to get your hound calmly out of whichever door, it's important he follows you, not you, him. Don't stop just because he has stopped. You choose where he can stop and sniff, you decide when to move on, even if he is mid sniff. (Once he's walking beautifully, you can slacken these rules, but to get the desired change you need to take control.) To get him moving again, just walk forward. You may want to add a "Let's go", and a small tug and release on the lead. Use the minimum force necessary. If your dog responds to a small tweak, no more effort is required. Other dogs will need a stronger lead correction.

If your dog pulls ahead rather than drags behind, wait for the lead to go taught, then give a little correction and an "Uhuh". Look ahead, not down at him, stand tall and lead like a leader, for he will be reading your body language. Relax your arms. Ideally you should be able to walk your dog at your side, on a slack lead that can be rested in the palm of your open hand.

To discourage zigzagging in front of you, make the lead shorter, so he has to trot by your side. Refrain from wrapping the lead around your hand as this causes tension your dog can read. Resist the urge to pull back on the lead. It will create an automatic reflex in the dog to pull against it.

Change direction often, and each time you do, give him a command to follow. I use "This way". Cross the road for no reason and then back again. Turn back on yourself for a few paces, then forward again. Be unpredictable so your dog has to listen and follow. If you always leave the house and take the exact same route to the park or on the school run, your dog will naturally be one step ahead. When you arrive at the park gates, walk past them, and then back again. Don't immediately let him off the lead when you arrive, to ricochet off. Instead let him off in a different spot every day. Once you remove the lead, have him wait until you give a release command. I use "OK".

Common Problems and How to Fix Them

Teaching puppies how to walk to heal on a loose lead needs a more encouraging approach, with more positive reinforcement. I deliver treats like a slot machine whilst walking forward. I mark and reward any eye contact or staying by my side. Sessions are kept short so as to maintain their focus. I would not advise on using lead corrections with a puppy.

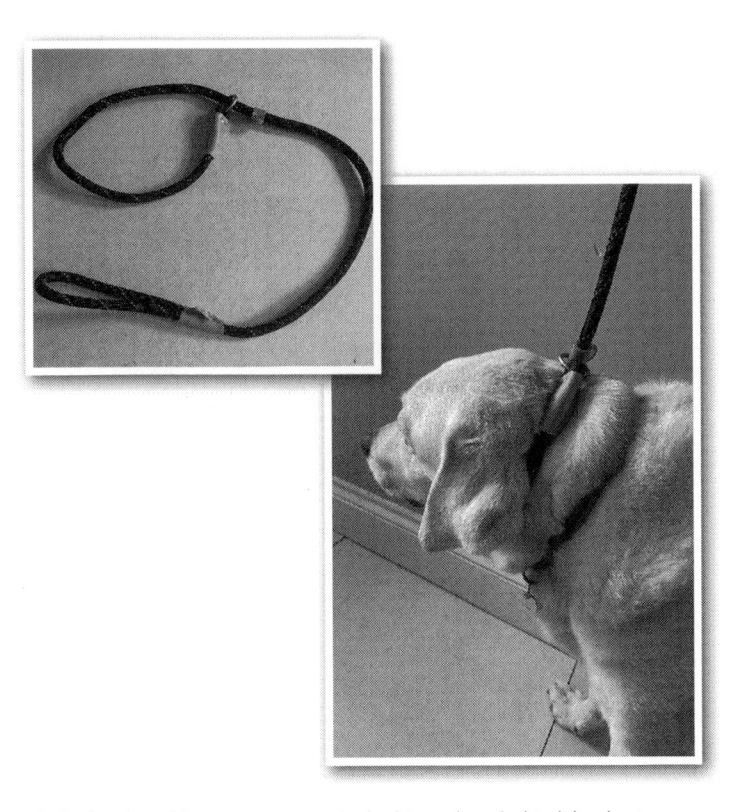

A slip lead, and how to position it, locked into place behind the dog's ears. No pressure on the windpipe. More control for the handler.

NO SUCH THING AS A BAD DOG

Training loose lead walking. You should be able to walk your dog with the lead draped loosely over an open hand. They should be at your side, mirroring your step.

Leaving the house, waiting respectfully in front of an open door. See how none of the dogs are standing in front of me. Leads are slack. The German shepherd was a house guest we (me, Willa and Rocky) were training. Dogs learn quicker from each other than from humans.

Case Study

Juno was a one year old springer spaniel. She had many insecurities which made her fearful of strangers, and occasionally defensively aggressive. She also had high separation anxiety and destructive tendencies when left alone. She was on edge when I entered the small apartment, so I suggested an immediate walk outside to relieve the tension. (Some conditions are exacerbated within four walls.) Her owners were a lovely young couple, newly married. Juno was their baby. And they had babied her from the start; never leaving her sight, and allowing her to do as she pleased. A dangerous combination.

They had actually got in touch because of the separation anxiety, but in order to deal with that, I had to build up trust between dog and owners first. And that meant cooperative, united lead walking. So off we went. I always observe first. What I saw was quite unexpected. This slightly nervous and unsure little dog threw off her mantle, barged past the three of us and rocketed down the communal stairs as soon as the door was opened a crack. This was the routine apparently. The owners had given up putting her on a lead as she had more than once pulled them over, one time resulting in a sprained ankle. The lady owner clipped Juno's very long lead on at the main entrance and wrapped it tightly round her hand. More barging through the door as we stepped outside, and immediate nose to the ground zigzagging and pulling. The owner was actually having to lean back, to counterbalance the dog's forward motion. The nose to the ground scenario was interspersed with walking just on two back feet, leaning as far forward as her owner was backwards.

I had seen all I needed to see. I required some time alone with this dog if I was going to earn her respect. Having her owners around was just going to reproduce the same bad energy, so I sent them off. I worked on getting Juno's eye contact with the help of my good friends Sausage and Chicken, and soon had her nose diverted off the floor and onto me. I switched their lead for a slip lead and began to change direction frequently, giving her the command "this way" every time, so she had something to follow. In true spaniel style, she almost immediately understood what I wanted from her, and paused every time I tweaked the lead. In under ten minutes I had her walking by my side on a slack lead, and took some video footage to prove it.

When the owners re-joined us, Juno, as is often the case when their owners are around, went back to pulling. That is what she does with *them*. It's a default switch that needs to be turned off. Juno had merely been responding to the energy the other end of the lead. I had shown them what Juno was capable of, so now it was time to train *them*.

Interestingly, my top three worst pullers have all been cocker or springer spaniels. Whether this is because they are such keenly driven dogs, or whether it is just coincidence, is hard to say. I suspect the former. In desperate cases, I have resorted to using the 'figure of eight' configuration, where the slip lead is twisted under the dog's chin and looped over his snout. It's the same idea as a halti head collar. If the dog surrenders to it and stops trying to get it off (distractions and treats used in abundance), for me, it has been 100% successful in stopping them from pulling. However, I don't continue if the dog is getting stressed by it. Ideally, I want the dog walking by my side because he chooses to, not because he is constrained to, so it's not a solution I revert to often.

Juno had proved she could walk nicely without the figure of eight lead, so now it was down to empowerment of the owners to change things around. They got there in fits and starts. Once Juno feels comfortable being left on her own, I'm confident the lead pulling will resolve itself completely, because it will mean she now has complete trust and respect for her owners.

CHAPTER 8
Recall

If you've ever been one of those people who stand in the park calling endlessly for your dog to come back, while he continues to play with his friends, chase those birds or sniff the ground, you will know how embarrassing and frustrating it is, especially if he looks up at you nonchalantly and then decides 'nah' and saunters off in the opposite direction, with little more than fresh air to divert his attention from you. It can be particularly annoying if you have some place to be. It can also be dangerous. Perhaps he has chased a deer over a barbed wire fence or a squirrel over the road.

Getting your dog to come back to you when you call should be one of the very first lessons you teach him. It begins in the house. This can be done as a puppy, a new rehomed dog or a dog you have had in the house for some years already. It's never too late to start over. I like to take part of a dog's daily food allowance in my hands and throw it piece by piece over the kitchen floor. He will gravitate back to me of his own accord for more.

Recall can be practised in stages:

- Let him smell what food you have in your hands. Throw a piece a few feet away. Let him run and get it. He should then come back to you for more. Throw another piece, let him get it and return to you. Repeat until the whole handful is gone. You have not given any commands, and yet the behaviour of returning to you is being hard-wired.
- Once he's got the hang of that, you can progress to the garden or an outside space with very little distraction, and do exactly the same. You can even increase the distance you throw the food.
- Next you can introduce calling his name, when he is on his way back to you. (If you are training with a whistle, give 3 short blows as he returns.) Note at this stage, the call is AS he is already running towards you, not before. Then you are guaranteed a 100% success rate.
- Introduce a visual cue. Put a treat in your hand and hold it in front of you, at knee level. As the dog reaches you, he will go straight for the treat. After a few repetitions, he will associate the hand gesture with a treat, even from a distance, and come running for it. Not just because the treat will be high value, something he never gets at any other time, but because he enjoys interacting with you and getting your praise.
- Take the recall game (for it should be perceived as a fun game) back into the house and this time go into another room so you are out of sight,

then call him. Reward him with a treat when he gets to you.
- Build on the previous point by hiding somewhere in the house, then calling him. He will have to work a bit harder to find you, but the reward will be extra satisfying for him when he finds you. Reward with lots of praise and/or a treat.
- Take the hiding recall game back outside where there are more smells and sights to distract him than inside, so you will need to up the value of the treats. I use chicken, cheese and sausage. Hide behind a bush or tree trunk, or in long grass and call his name.
- If there are two or more of you, stand some distance apart and take turns in calling him to you. Reward with praise and a treat when he reaches you. He should find this a really fun game. If you can remain more fun than your surroundings, then you will have a higher chance of him returning to you.
- I use a long line when training recall in more stubborn dogs. It prevents the dog from ever getting it wrong or ignoring. If he doesn't respond when I call, I give a short tug and release on the lead, which starts his forward motion. Greater success is achieved if you move backwards, as you call, or say "This way" to signal you are changing direction and moving on. Dogs love to follow and chase. If you are standing still when you call, he may be thinking, "Why should I come? You're not going anywhere".

- Continue with the long line in more and more distracting environments. Never let him get so stuck into his environment that you become 'invisible' to him. Call him back often. Make eye contact often, to reconnect with him.
- Once coming back 100% of the time, you are now ready to let him off the long line. Still call him back to you often, and occasionally put the short lead back on. Walk for a few minutes on the short lead, **then let him off again**. Reason being, you don't want him to associate putting the lead on with the end of the walk, or he will be less likely to return. If the lead going on means another loop of the park, how much happier he will be to return to you.
- Always feed after the walk. Dogs like having a purpose and should be made to work for their food. More importantly, it gives them a reason to go home. Also, if they've built up an appetite, they'll be more likely to eat a full meal (if you have a fussy eater) and with a full belly, then be in a restful state for a few hours to let you get on with your chores.
- NEVER scold when your dog returns to you – even if he has ignored your frantic calls to come back for over an hour. You will only be teaching him not to come back to you the next time. Dogs live in the moment and they can't associate a past event (choosing to ignore your call) with a present one (responding to your call and being back at your side), so if he is punished when he

finally returns and runs up to you, he won't be doing that again!
- With time, eke out the number of treats you give. Switch to just praise every other time instead. Eventually just produce a treat on the odd random occasion.

Remember, the walk is not passive. You need to be repeatedly engaging with your dog. Throw him a ball a couple of times (then put it away, keep it powerful), hide some treats around a tree trunk, get him to jump onto a tree stump to find a delicious treat there. Be animated and full of praise. If you are the most interesting thing out there, you should have no problem with recall.

Case Study

I'm going to use my own dog Rocky as a less than perfect example here. I adopted him when he was around 3 years old, from a Romanian rescue centre. He arrived with a host of insecurities and I discovered later, some pretty intense prey drive. I worked on bonding exercises daily, so that by the time I was ready to let him off the lead, I knew he would come back. The rescue centre recommended at least 6 weeks of remaining on the lead, for trust to build. I let him off after two. Exactly the opposite of what I tell my clients! "Never move on to stage two before you have 100% per cent success rate with stage one." But hey, I'm a behaviourist, and I was keen to put in the work and see progress. In fact, Rocky was very responsive coming back to me in London parks. He felt safer by my side, than out in the open surrounded by the noise, unpredictability and busyness of the city. It was when we arrived in the countryside that his confidence set in, and he felt at ease, getting stuck into all the smells the landscape had to offer. My high value chicken and sausage were shunned in favour of country smells, so I had to hope that the work we had put in at home, playing games, would make me attractive enough for him to come back to. I had enrolled on an online course called 'Sexier Than A Squirrel', which guided you through many fun things to do with your dog to make him more interested in you than chasing squirrels. It had worked up until now.

I loved watching him dive into the bushes to hunt out a rabbit or a pheasant, and it was a joy to see him relaxed for once, and having so much fun. For this reason, I allowed him to run off. I did not call him as he hightailed it into the undergrowth, for I knew he would not turn around midchase, and he would be only practising ignoring me. Instead, I kept moving and would occasionally call "Rocky, this way", which is what he knew signalled that we were moving on. If you call your dog from a stationary position, why should he come when he knows you will still be there in 5 or 10 minutes' time? He will finish his digging or chasing and then return to you in his own good time. If he knows you are moving away, however, and your call is getting fainter and fainter, he won't want to be left behind, so will be more likely to come before he is ready to. The reason I don't call his name repeatedly is because I don't want to become white noise which is easy to ignore. The occasional 'Rocky!' puncturing the silence is more powerful.

One year on and Rocky does always come back, but sometimes not immediately. There have been a couple of incidents where I have walked all the way back to the car or house (no roads to cross I hasten to add) and waited there for 15 minutes until he appeared. I still, through slightly gritted teeth, had praise for him when he returned. Because I allowed the prey seeking behaviour in the first place, I created the end product. If I wanted to, I could start over, and put him back on the long lead, but I am actually happier managing the behaviour rather than eradicating it. He is getting to release some of his natural urges, and I get to witness a happy hound.

CHAPTER 9
Prey Drive and Chasing

This chapter is closely linked to the previous one on recall. Chances are, if your dog has prey drive, his recall is pretty poor or selective at least. Prey drive is the instinctive inclination to pursue and capture/kill prey. Dogs are born with it. Working dogs such as sight hounds and scent hounds have been bred to heighten these instincts. Lurchers, greyhounds, whippets, salukis, to name a few sighthounds, use their vision to seek out prey and then give chase. Foxhounds, bloodhounds, beagles, basset hounds, to name a few scent hounds, use their noses to follow the scent of prey. Terriers and herding breeds (eg collies, heelers, Old English sheepdogs) and hunting/sporting breeds (eg spaniels, retrievers, pointers, dachshunds) are also driven by their natural instincts to hunt, chase and corral other animals. So it is no surprise that prey drive is a common issue.

In the wild, the drive to seek and kill prey is paramount for survival. In domesticity, this drive is considered a 'problem'. Your neighbour would not take kindly to your dog chasing their cat. A farmer has a legal right to shoot any dog chasing his sheep. But is it really fair to expect to eradicate a perfectly natural hard-wired behaviour? More often than not, it can't be eradicated, but it can be managed. You may think that removing the prey would remove the drive. Not so. The absence of pheasants, vermin, sheep, cattle etc, does not mean that the drive to chase disappears. Instead, it is transferred onto children, bikes, cars, joggers etc. Anything that moves is fair game.

The way I deal with a chasing issue is fourfold. One, work on recall. Two, give the dog a controlled outlet for its drive to hunt and chase. Three, work on the bond between the two of you, so you become more fascinating than a squirrel. Four, praise and reward the dog for ignoring the prey. This is a form of counter conditioning which creates new positive neural pathways. The idea is that your dog will get more of a dopamine hit looking to you to play that game, or get that reward, than he would from chasing that prey. If your dog is chasing for the mere fun of it, and not due to some predatory urge, your job will be all the easier, just by taking the fun out of it. A simple 'no' should suffice, along with a lead correction (assuming he is on a long line), and then redirect his focus onto you with whatever action works for him.

Let me expand on the above four points:
1. Work on recall: see chapter 8 for how to do this.
2. Give the dog an outlet for his prey drive: if you prevent him from running after prey, then you need to give him an alternative, to satisfy that craving. Take him into a space free from distraction – an open field or your back garden – and play chase with him. You can even do it around your kitchen table. Or throw him a ball

or frisbee. Chuck the ball into bushes so he has to spend some time sniffing it out. But use these toys sparingly. You do not want to create an obsession, and you do not want him to get bored of them. Throw a few times, then put away. I have a clever little tool called a flirt pole, which is a ragged rope on the end of piece of string, attached to a pole. A bit like a fishing rod. Cats have similar poles with feathers on the end. The rope wriggles around like a mouse when you shake the pole, and a prey driven dog will just have to get his paws on it. You can drain the dog with very little movement from yourself, although I prefer to animate myself by running all over the place. If he catches the rope, trade the rope for a treat, so he drops it willingly. Do not enter into a game of tug-of-war, and do not let him shake the rope, as this is him practising 'killing' the toy.

3. Work on the bond between the two of you: the more you play with your dog, the more he will want to be around you. And if he loves being around you, he will be less inclined to slope off looking for prey. Play games inside as well as out (there is a list of ideas in chapter 22 on Mental Stimulation). Keep calling him back to you regularly when out on a walk, reconnect, get eye contact, chuck a treat for him to sniff out. Don't let him get too stuck into his surroundings.

4. Praise and reward for ignoring the prey: this needs to be practised in a very controlled environment. Start easy so the dog knows what

is expected of him. With your dog on a short lead, and if possible, wildlife behind a fence (I'm going to use sheep as an example), approach from a distance. You will see from your dog's body language, when he has noticed the sheep; ears pricked, staring at them, stiff body, mouth closed, perhaps low to the ground in a stalking position. Allow him to notice them and then distract him. A piece of chicken or liver cake under the nose usually works well. But don't give him the chicken yet. Use it to turn his head away from the sheep. Get his attention so he looks up at you. As soon as his eyes meet yours, say "Yes" (or click if using a clicker), and reward by throwing the chicken for him to sniff out. Do not approach the sheep any closer until you have done this a few times. Then repeat the steps a little closer. Then move away and continue your walk. Keeping it short will stop the urge to chase building up. You have left on success and sown the seeds of a new behaviour. Repeat for a few days before you do the same manoeuvres a little closer. If at any point he takes a lunge towards the sheep, say "No" or "Uhuh", as I prefer, with a little lead correction, and back away. The combination of negative and positive reinforcement will teach him new behaviour. He will soon learn that lunging will get him his owner's displeasure, and take him further from the sheep, whilst not reacting will get him a reward.

Do not expect overnight success. Repetition and consistency are key. You will get better results if your dog has drained some energy before doing this exercise. If he's fresh out the blocks after a good night's sleep, you may be setting yourself up to fail.

Once your dog is successfully looking to you every time you ask, when in front of the sheep, you are ready to progress to walking him on a long line through a field of sheep. Call him back to you before he ever reaches the end of the line. The line should never go taut. The only time it should go taut is if he has ignored your call to return, and hence given himself a correction as he reaches the full length of the line.

CHAPTER 10
Obsessions

Dog obsessions are many and varied, and can include fixating on a ball, toy or even sticks or stones, tail chasing, staring at reflections, self-licking, carpet (or other object) licking, staring and barking repeatedly at the same thing, pacing.

Whatever the obsession, you can be sure it stemmed from a circumstance that was forced upon the dog. Dogs do not deliberately choose to obsess over things. There are no obsessions in the wild, demonstrating that left to their own devices, animals live balanced, harmonious lives. Only in captivity do the strange behaviours start to emerge. (Think of a pacing leopard in a zoo.) Obsessions begin as a coping strategy, most often when suffering from stress. In my experience, that stress is broadly a lack of stimulation. It's for this reason that high-energy dogs or intelligent breeds seem to suffer the most.

As with every condition, each case must be viewed individually, and a programme of rehabilitation should be designed for that particular dog. But broadly speaking, I would firstly rule out any medical reason the dog was acting compulsively, then asses the root cause. If the cause was boredom and stress, I would recommend more physical and mental exercise. At the same time, the dog would need to be trained out of his fixation, and that often means telling him "No", and redirecting him onto another activity.

Border collies frequently come up in this category because of their impressive brain power. They are working dogs, and when raised in a family home with no job to do, they can resort to finding themselves something to do which relates to their herding instincts. I have seen collies who will chase light reflections, in an attempt to herd them into one place. I have seen them round up a bunch of children in their attempts to fulfil their natural urges and I have seen collies who stare at their reflections in puddles, glass windows and mirrors, not because they like looking at themselves, but because they have worked out that it gets their owners' attention. Similarly, I have heard of collies staring at the same spot on the ceiling for the same reason. Collies are also very ball fixated. Please do not feed this obsession if you can relate, but instead, give him a healthy way to release his natural instinct, by taking him to agility classes or playing loads of varied activity and brain games.

It is normal to start throwing balls for your dog when he is young. After all, they enjoy a healthy game of catch and chase, and they are also getting some physical exercise. Problems can arise when this ball throwing is used as a quick fix to exercise your high-drive dog, and used in place of a walk. The dog gets more and more stimulated, and becomes fitter and fitter, and before you know it, you have a ball-obsessed dog on your hands who has no off switch, and no matter how much exercise you give him, he will not tire. By all means throw a few balls for your dog in the early days, but stop it after a few throws and let the dog sniff and follow you.

If he persistently demands the ball, stop taking it on walks altogether. Introduce a variety of other activities for him – sensory games, hiding games, sniffing games. (See chapter 22: Mental Stimulation.)

Case Study

Milly was a young flat-coated retriever, owned by some very dear friends of mine. I noticed her peculiar behaviour when visiting for lunch. As I pulled into the drive and got out of the car, she promptly dropped a stone at my feet. No hello-nice-to-see-you waggle, sniff or eye contact. Just 'plop, here's a stone for you'. I ignored her and went inside. I was not going to engage in this type of behaviour. However, I noticed as the other guests arrived, that she tried her luck with them, and was rewarded. Some of them threw the stone for her to fetch, while others laughed and stroked her. Essentially praising her for her actions.

As the day drew out, her behaviour became more intense. She found balls and stones and dropped them at anyone's feet, not withdrawing her eyes from the offering at any stage. At one point I took away all the balls I could find lying about – and there were plenty – and hid them from her. Not dissuaded, she went and found another, and when I hid that one, another still. For the entire 5 hours I was there, she was fixated, staring at a ball or stone. It upset me to see her in this state, and I broached the subject with her owners.

"Oh yes, she's totally mad – loves a ball!".

"But do you realise this is wholly unnatural and is an unhealthy obsession?"

"Yes, she is rather obsessed I supposed, hahaha!"

"Seriously, this is not good for her health. It's putting a lot of untold strain on her system."

"Oh."

I persuaded them to let me come back and have a session with her, without charge. I was just embarking on my career as a dog behaviourist, so it was going to be an interesting challenge.

My friends, Milly's owners, had a generous garden, and the dogs were free to roam as they pleased, and also were taken on the occasional walk. I tried to explain that the garden was no substitute for a structured walk, whereby the dogs could experience different smells and surroundings, and take direction from their human pack leader. Milly was not getting the outlet she needed for her retrieving self. There were no rules in the house, as far as I could see, and the dogs were left to their own devices. This is a dangerous concoction for a clever, working breed.

My first job was to drain some of Milly's physical energy. It was the afternoon, and she had not been taken on a walk yet. I tied her to my scooter and made her run beside me for about twenty minutes. I then did some short lead exercises with her, giving her a command to follow each time I turned direction. I needed her focus on me, so worked on getting eye contact every time I stopped, by wafting the smell of chicken under her nose. This had the desired effect of getting her to look up at me, and then I gave her the reward.

I then repeated the same short lead exercises with a ball on the ground. If she stared at the ball, I gave a short tug on the lead. If she looked up at me, I gave a reward. She soon worked out that it was more favourable to ignore the ball and look up at me. I increased the challenge by placing several balls around the lawn, and walked her over every one of them. She was a superstar and soon ignored every one. Not bad for a dog who had been practising ball obsession for the last four years.

It was at this point that I called on my friend to join us. I normally work the dog with the owner present, but my friend represented excitement to Milly, so I had to remove her in order to get a new habit established. I demonstrated how Milly was able to ignore the balls scattered around the place, and even threw a few for good measure. With very little prompting Milly ignored them, and eventually lay down to relax. Soft focus. Totally spent, mentally and physically.

To be honest, I wasn't sure what I would be able to achieve that day, as this was my first obsession case, but I can tell you, I was pretty chuffed with the snapshot I took before I left, of Milly staring peacefully into space, relaxed body language, surrounded by balls, sitting on the stony driveway. I texted the photo to the husband, who replied, "Trick photography?"

Milly, after our training session, relaxed and ignoring the balls.

CHAPTER 11
Separation Anxiety

Dogs are pack animals. Once upon a time they all lived in the wild. They travelled together, slept together, hunted together or waited together for their mother to return from hunting. Togetherness is engrained in their psyches. It is therefore totally unnatural for them to sit alone for much of the day. Yet that is what we expect them to do. In order to pave the way in a gentle and considerate manner, we should, where possible, mould them from puppyhood. This means leaving them for short periods of time on their own while they are still young. I would never recommend leaving a pup alone in his crate to cry it out. He needs to know that you will be there to help and comfort him if he is in distress. But, never leaving your pup's side may create separation problems further down the line. If he gets up and walks away from you, let him. He is asking for space. So often we follow our pups around constantly, waiting for them to pee or poised to stop them eating something they shouldn't, while we should be allowing them a little independence. Encourage nap times in a crate on their own. You could be pottering around in the same room at first, but over time and moving at a speed the puppy is comfortable with, make sure you leave the room for short periods. This will get them accustomed to being on their own whilst **in a calm frame of mind.**

If a dog is left on their own in a state of anxiety, destructiveness may ensue. (See the following chapter.) You may find your door scratched to pieces, marking the dog's desperate attempts to get to the other side. Chewing alleviates stress, so you could find your furniture is in pieces as well as the door frame. In addition, a really stressed-out dog will lose sphincter control, and add yet more mess to the place. Owners without this knowledge may come home and scold the dog, making him more anxious, and therefore more likely to cause a mess the next time he is left on his own. **He hasn't been naughty – he's just trying to tell you something.**

I have found that the majority of separation anxiety cases I deal with stem from the dog sleeping on the owner's bed. I'm not saying this isn't a lovely natural bonding way to behave, but I am saying know the risks, especially if you have a breed which is more prone to becoming distressed away from their owners. I believe it is kinder in the long run to set your dog up with being comfortable sleeping away from you. Ideally in a separate room.

Certain breeds which are particularly prone to separation anxiety, include those which were bred for companionship, such as lap dogs like the bichon frise, Chihuahua, cavalier King Charles spaniel and toy poodle. But larger breeds can suffer too; Australian shepherds, and German shepherds seem to struggle particularly.

But the problem is not breed-dependant. Any dog can suffer from separation anxiety, through improper training. If

Common Problems and How to Fix Them

you find yourself in this camp, or if you have adopted a dog with separation issues, there are several things you can do to alleviate them:

1. Build confidence. Practise periods of separation from him, before you actually leave him on his own for the first time. If he always has to be touching you, this could simply mean sitting at (not on) your feet, instead of on your lap. Then see if you can sit across the room from him, putting him back on his bed every time he gets off. If he follows you from room to room, ask him to stay on his bed in one room, while you move to a room next door, where he can still smell and hear you. (Look at chapter 24 on impulse control to help with this.) I wouldn't advise allowing your dog to sleep on your bed, for how will this prepare him to be able to sleep on his own when you leave the house?

2. Crate training is useful for learning to be comfortable with separation. Dogs are denning animals, and the crate is like a cosy safe space for them. Another bonus of using a crate is that dogs will seldom soil their sleeping areas, and they will be unable to pace. Pacing is born of stress, but if the body can't pace, the mind relaxes. The crate should be big enough for the dog to stand up and turn around in. Any bigger and he may soil one end of it. Make sure the crate is introduced in a positive way, so it represents relaxation. Invite your dog to eat and rest in the crate with

the door closed. You can be in the same room initially. As the days progress leave the room for a few minutes at a time, gradually lengthening the time you are away. Walk out the front door, wait a few seconds, then come in again. Build on this. Always wait for quiet before opening the crate, even if it's only a few seconds between whines. Don't let him rush out when you open the door. Open the door, but block the exit with your body. Wait for calm and an absence of pushing forward, then get up and move away. You are always rewarding calm behaviour. Do not knowingly leave him howling for hours in the crate or it will start to represent anxiousness for him.

If your dog is anxious about the crate because he has had a bad past experience related to it, you can still reintroduce it, but slowly and sensitively. When it first arrives, just leave the crate in the room with the door open for a few days, so it becomes part of the furniture. Make it comfortable inside, maybe with something that smells of you for comfort. Throw in some toys and treats. Allow the dog to go in and retrieve them, and come straight out again. You can stuff a Kong (rubber toy) with treats and tie it to the back of the crate, so the dog has to remain in the crate if he wants to eat what's inside the Kong. After a long walk, so he's tired, start feeding meals in the crate. Only after the dog is comfortable with entering of his own accord, should you then

Common Problems and How to Fix Them

block his exit when he has finished eating. You can crouch down and block with your body, or an arm across the doorway. When he gives up trying to push through, just get up and move away. No words. You are having a conversation the dog way. Days or weeks later, you can progress to closing the door while he eats his meal in the crate. With a full belly, and exhausted from the long walk you gave him beforehand, you may find he lies down and goes to sleep. But don't push your luck. Open the door after 10 minutes or so. He may even choose to stay in there, as you have successfully made the crate represent relaxation. It's also important that he is never bothered in there – no young children crawling in with him, no poking him through the bars. He must view it as his safe space.

3. Give your dog a long walk before leaving him on his own. He will then be in a more restful state (and will not need to toilet).
4. Leave him with something to chew on. The very act of chewing triggers the release of endorphins, which have a calming effect. As such, your dog is self-medicating for stress. He may even look forward to you leaving, as that's when the big treats come out. Be sure to also provide chews when you are not about to leave too, in case the appearance of a chew triggers the anticipation of you leaving.
5. Leave him with something that smells of you; a sweaty T-shirt or old slipper he can chew on.

He'll find it comforting to be surrounded by your smell.

6. Never make a big deal of coming and going. Don't say goodbye with a sad face, which will only make your dog think there is something to worry about. Maybe chuck a bit of his kibble over the kitchen floor, and just walk out, letting him get on with hunting the bits out. When you come home don't go ballistic at seeing him again, as good as that will make *you* feel. You will just be teaching him that there should be a huge difference in his state of mind between you not being there, and you being there. Say hello softly once you have hung your coat up.

7. Practise fake goodbyes. Pick up your keys, put on your coat, walk round the house, then sit down again. Anxiety starts to build as soon as he sees these triggers, if he associates them with you walking out the door. You can stop that anxiety rising by being unpredictable about your departures.

8. Add soothing aids to the environment. There are various plug-in diffusers, sprays and collars on the market which claim to help settle your dog, by releasing synthetic pheromones into the atmosphere. There are also specialised soundtracks on YouTube compiled to help soothe anxious dogs. I would be wary about leaving the TV or radio on, as you never know what sounds might appear, and it might cause more harm than good.

9. If possible, leave your dog for short periods of time with a friend or family member, or a dog walker. This way he gets used to not always having you around.

Case Study

Mahler was an 18-month-old cockapoo with severe separation anxiety. His owner called me after the first UK COVID lockdown, when she had gone back to work. It was a familiar call I was getting. Dogs who had had their owners present 24 hours a day, working from home for months, were suddenly subjected to long absences as the humans returned to work. When Mahler's owner returned from work for the first time, post lockdown, she walked into the kitchen to find the dog bed pulled from its crate and shredded, stuffing all over the floor, chairs upturned, the inside of the kitchen door scratched and door frame chewed, and Mahler bleeding from the mouth. He had only been on his own for a few hours. She promptly rang me, and set up a pet cam in the meantime.

Watching the footage was revealing and distressing. As soon as the front door closed, Mahler jumped onto a chair and then onto the kitchen table. From here he had an elevated view through the glass-paned kitchen double doors and out of the window beyond, onto the street. He then alternated between scratching furiously at the door, pacing, whining, barking and chewing on whatever was lying around. He didn't sit still once in two hours. No wonder he slept so well all afternoon once his owner returned.

Mahler's owner, let's call her Nancy, had 'inherited' him from a work colleague who didn't have the time to walk him, and who was not willing to put in the training required to keep a high-energy dog. She had looked after Mahler for a few days in the past, and those days turned into weeks, until she was offered full custody. The work colleague used to leave Mahler at home for most of the working day, so Nancy was relieved that at last she could offer Mahler a stable home, where her mum could look after him when she (Nancy) was at work. Recently however, Nancy's mum had become ill, and was unable to dog-sit, so Nancy was popping in from work every few hours to let him out.

It seemed to me like Mahler had had a bad experience of being left on his own before, with his previous owner, and so when left on his own again, it triggered bad memories and a feeling of anxiety. Coupled with Nancy going back to work, having had her at home and all to himself for the last eight weeks, this was a killer blow.

We started by reintroducing the crate in a positive way, throwing treats in there, which he went in to get, leaving the door open, yet asking him to stay in there as we chatted. Every time his head popped out, I walked toward him and told him, "On your bed". After a couple of prompts he was happy to lie there relaxing. I rewarded him with a couple of treats. Good start.

We then edged out of the room, having told him "Stay", still chatting so he could hear us. I stood near the doorway so I could just see him, and every time he tried to leave the crate I repeated, "On your bed". We had to do this several times until he stayed put, and when he did, I went back in and rewarded him. We repeated several times. This was to be Nancy's homework for the next week. The reason I left the crate door open was so he could learn some impulse control.

Common Problems and How to Fix Them

He was *choosing* to stay in there, rather being constrained to do so. Often, when a dog is behind a barrier, he just has an urge to get to the other side. Along with the staying on his bed, Nancy was to put into practise all the above 9 points. No need for me to repeat them here.

On my second visit, seeing they had totally nailed step 1, we repeated the ritual, but this time left the house for 3 seconds, and re-entered. I rewarded only when Mahler stayed in his crate and did not come out to greet us. This was the homework for the second week, slowly eking out the time spent behind the front door, but never making it so long that he failed and left his bed, or came to the front door.

Nancy also had a problem with the nights. She had been unable to leave Mahler on his own in the kitchen, without him protesting, since going back to work. He had been in his crate beside her bed. With his new found confidence, I thought him ready for a little separation there as well. I told Nancy to put his crate just outside the bedroom, with the bedroom door open, crate door closed. She reported no protests the following day. After a week I suggested she move the crate to the landing half way down the stairs. Still no protest. After another week the crate was moved to the bottom of the stairs, and a week after that, to the kitchen. It was important not to move him on too quickly, as I didn't want to have to take a step back, or make him fail. The more nights in a row he could accomplish without getting upset, the more this would become his new default setting. Anyway, he seemed happy with the rate of progression from bedroom to kitchen, and now sleeps there quite happily.

Weeks later Nancy reported that she had watched Mahler on the pet cam after she left, calmly gnawing on a chew, on his bed. Then he sauntered around the kitchen, took a drink, and then settled back down to sleep.

There have been setbacks, as I would have expected. But these setbacks were always related to something Nancy did or didn't do. For example, if she hadn't had time to give him a long walk before leaving him, he didn't manage as well. She freely admitted that some days she lapsed on the rules, not following through if Mahler came off his bed when she had asked him stay. But I had demonstrated that the dog was capable. The rest was down to her.

Mahler on one of our training walks, accompanied by Rocky and Willa.

CHAPTER 12
Destructiveness

Have you ever come home to find your skirting boards gnawed, your scatter cushions emptied of filling or your carpet shredded? If you have, the next thing you have probably done is shout at your dog. He will probably cower and look 'guilty' with those whale eyes of his, and you will conclude that he knows he has done wrong.

Contrary to belief, showing the whites of his eyes with a lowered or turned head, whilst looking directly at you (whale eye), is his reaction to your behaviour. It is an appeasement gesture. He is anticipating trouble and his body language is one of submission. He is most likely stressed and fearful.

The only guilty party in this scenario is the owner. If I came home to such a scene, my reaction would be, "What have I done to make my dog so stressed?" I would feel an immediate apology coming on.

Dogs are destructive for several reasons, but more often than not, it is because they are bored or stressed at being left alone. Destructiveness is often linked with separation anxiety, so I have intentionally linked this chapter to the previous one. Bored dogs who are not given enough mental or physical exercise will find other ways of draining their energy, and this may include chewing up the house. Dogs who are stressed or anxious find that the act of chewing releases endorphins, which actively calms them. Other possible causes could be hunger, health problems (especially if the destructiveness is aimed at himself, such as paw chewing) or in younger dogs, teething.

There are very simple ways to cure destructiveness:

1. Spend as much time as you can interacting with your dog, and give him lots of mental exercise and brain games.
2. Make sure he is properly exercised physically. I recommend at least 1 ½ hours daily split into either end of the day, on and off lead if possible. Obviously, older or infirm dogs may need much less.
3. Hire a dog walker to take the dog out while you are away, or pop home often to interact with your dog throughout the day. Alternatively, book him into day care. If you can do none of these due to time restrictions or financial restraints, I'm sorry, but the bottom line is, you shouldn't have a dog.
4. Teach relaxation in a crate. (I explain in chapter 11 how to introduce a crate properly.) However, I for one would not leave a dog in a crate for long periods during the day. Two hours max.
5. Leave the TV on so he doesn't feel so alone.
6. Try calming sprays and collars, and pheromone diffusers.

7. Leave him something he CAN chew on.
8. Thunder shirts and body wraps help calm some dogs.
9. Do not leave your dog alone for longer than he can cope with. Keep your outings short at first and gradually increase over time once you know he is not stressed. Install a pet cam if necessary so you can monitor at which point he goes over threshold.

Destructiveness in the garden amounts to the same thing. Digging holes, chewing up flowerbeds etc, is your dog finding ways to amuse himself, due to lack of any other stimulation, or not enough of it. The garden is just an extension of the house, and no substitute for going for a walk, which *is* stimulation.

Case Study

A lovely young Brazilian couple called on me to help them with their 8-month-old Samoyed, Ava. Ava is short for Avalanche. Her older Samoyed companion is called Tufao. (Typhoon in English). Ava, for one, certainly lived up to her name and left a huge mess in her wake whenever her owners left the house. Tufao was the more stable of the two, but his steady demeanour didn't seem to have any calming effect on her. I was shown photos of shredded magazines, frayed rugs and bleeding gums. The chewed skirting boards and scratched front door were plain for me to see. Here was one distressed little lady.

Ava's owner worked long hours in A&E for the NHS, so she was well versed in taking control and dealing with emergency situations with a level head. She had pretty good control of the dogs in the house: she gave a command, they obeyed. Out of the house she responded beautifully to my training, and she soon resolved the lead pulling. What she lacked was time. Time to interact with the dogs. Time to walk the dogs. Young dogs especially, need lots of mental stimulation to drain all that exuberant energy. Samoyeds are renowned for needing bags of exercise. Here's what Google says about them:

> *"This playful dog enjoys vigorous outdoor exercise, especially in cold weather. Without such outlets for his energy, and without sufficient companionship to satisfy his sociable nature, he can be boisterous and destructive."*

It's always wise to research a breed's needs before buying. I don't mean to be judgemental in this particular case – I have no idea about the acquisition situation – just something for the reader to think about.

Ava was being left on her own (by that I mean no human companionship) for long periods, having not been walked first. She had free rein of the house when left, so everything was a target for destruction. Nothing puppy-proofed. This was a disaster waiting to happen.

Ava's owner felt it mean to crate her, but in fact, in this case it would have been kinder to crate, than imposing no boundaries at all. When the body isn't pacing, the mind calms down, so physically stopping movement can often help a dog to relax. Crating was going to be a last resort, as it had been introduced wrongly when Ava was younger, and she now had negative associations with it. And if Ava picked up any vibes that her owner was feeling sorry for her, as she locked her in, then it really wasn't going to work anyway.

My prescription was simple: short walks spread several times throughout the day to alleviate boredom, and a long one before being left in the morning; start to leave her for short periods only, and build from there; mental stimulation in the form of puzzles, interactive owner/dog games; varying feeding methods (as taking food out of a bowl on the floor is just plain boring). I suggested leaving her closed in the kitchen – she loved lying on the tiled kitchen floor to cool – with lots of toys she *could* chew on.

As long as the lengthy morning walks were actioned, the destruction stayed mostly at bay. When timing was an issue, or when it was raining (it was the owners, not the dogs who wouldn't go out in the rain), then I suggested more brain games to tire Ava out instead.

This is the photo Ava's owner sent me when first asking for my help.

CHAPTER 13
Fear

Fearfulness does have a place in the dog world. It is a built-in instinct which keeps them away from danger. However, some dogs are more scared than is natural. Let's look at some of the reasons your dog could be scared:

1. Nature. Dogs born to nervous mothers will be predisposed to developing similar traits.
2. Pain. Dogs that are 'hand shy' may be protecting themselves from being touched due to some underlying health condition.
3. Traumatic experiences. Weeks 8-12 of a puppy's life are known as the fear imprint stage. Any traumatic experience during this stage can have lasting effects for the rest of his life. It is important that all experiences during this stage are positive. Even later in life, a single scary experience can create a lifelong fear response. For example, if a dog is startled by a firecracker, he may grow to associate all loud noises with fear. He will remember the place he heard

the firecracker, and may become fearful on revisiting that place.
4. Poor socialisation. Puppies between the age of 8-16 weeks need positive exposure to a variety of people, animals, places, noises, handling. They need plenty of pleasant interactions with the world around them in order to grow into confident young adults.
5. Puberty. Between 6-12 months of age young dogs have a hormone surge. This can result in some slight behaviour changes. They can develop a fear of previously familiar things and situations. It may begin as something they are merely unsure about, but the owner's reaction to the dog will determine whether that unsureness develops into full blown fear.

What to do? Firstly, it is important to be able to recognise when your dog is going through a stressful or frightening moment. Take a look at the list of body language **stress signals** in chapter 25 on communication.

Anyone with a fearful dog will know how crippling it can be for them (the dogs). The urge to comfort and soothe, as we would a fellow human, is overwhelming. However, and this is the biggest mistake I see, giving affection to a dog in an anxious state of mind, is nurturing that fearful state. The dog understands that affection is a reward, so receiving a caress and soft words when he is scared, means he is being rewarded for feeling afraid in that moment. The result being that you will increase his fear. Dogs do not need love when they are afraid. They need leadership. I often tell my clients to adopt a school mistressy manner to restore confidence, "Spit spot. Come along now, don't be so silly".

Another way us humans can actually make fear worse in a dog is by becoming scared ourselves. Imagine that your dog reacts fearfully to a noisy skateboard. The next time you see a skateboard, you tense up, predicting that your dog will react. Your dog, sensing your anxiousness, becomes even more scared, as there is obviously something to be worried about, and a vicious cycle begins. If there is no escape (a fearful dog would choose to flee if he could) because he is on a lead, then he may be forced to pass by this 'threatening' skateboard, and the only defence left to him is to fight, to see off the danger, and protect himself and his human. This is how humans can turn a fearful dog into an aggressive dog. The dog's natural reaction is to take over, in the absence of leadership.

Dogs exhibit allelomimetic behaviour. This means that they learn by imitating. This is why remaining calm and assertive is the key to getting them over that fear. If they see that you aren't scared by the noisy passing skateboard, it will make them more confident. If their owner is ignoring the scary thing, then maybe it isn't that scary after all.

An analogy that helps, is to imagine you are on a plane when you hit some bad turbulence. (I, for one, hate flying, especially turbulence.) Now, if you looked at the cabin crew and they were all shaking in their boots, you would feel even more anxious, wouldn't you? But if they were perfectly calm, and told you to go and sit down, after all it's just a bit of turbulence, wouldn't you would feel more relaxed, and trust that they had everything under control?

Common things dogs are scared of include loud noises, children (they can be noisy and very unpredictable), going outside, men, strangers, other dogs, traffic, people holding anything resembling a stick, going in the car, new situations etc. But the list is endless really and can grow to include all sorts of things if you react wrongly. It is very hard to give a generic formula for dealing with fear. Each dog is different and so is their particular fear. But one thing is definitely needed, and that is patience. It can take years to turn a dog around. Sometimes the fear is so ingrained it can only be managed, and not cured.

Ex-street dogs are particularly scarred. We have no idea what they might have endured. My own came to me around the age of three, from Romania. The journey itself must have been very stressful. He spent a week in a kill shelter before being rescued by a British charity and brought to England. He was neutered and treated for heartworm which took 6 months to clear. He had to have his teeth scaled under general anaesthetic, and three teeth extracted when I got him as they were completely rotten. Considering all this, he never showed a fear of going to the vet, which is a great credit to our veterinary practitioners. He spent the first few weeks hiding under bushes in the garden, or in a corner of the kitchen, making himself as small as possible. He would not go through a doorway if I was holding the door. Presumably he had had a few closed on him in the past, intentionally or otherwise. On the street, he would make a dash for the nearest car and curl up underneath it. He was very jumpy around traffic, wary of all men, and terrified of any loud bangs, no matter how distant. On day one, he bit my husband, and after a few weeks (once he felt settled in his new home) he started to bark and lunge at anyone that came into the house. I could write a whole book on him alone. He could be a case study for most of the chapters in this book. Much aggression is born of fear, and I shall write more on this in the following chapter.

A fearful dog needs to know that you will protect him. First, you have to build up a level of trust. This starts with clear leadership and guidance. Always be calm and assertive. You may have to develop a more gentle assertiveness with fearful dogs. Walk him passively away from situations which stress him. Stand between him and what he fears. For example, if he is scared of traffic then always walk him on the side furthest from the road, so your body is between him and the traffic. If he is scared of other dogs, stand between him and the other dog. Once he trusts you to keep him safe, then you can start working on reintroducing his triggers carefully and in a controlled environment. If you took everything that scared your dog away from him, yes you are helping him short term, but his world would become very small, and he would still react with fear if faced with those fears again. I like to change a dog's perception, so something he once found terrifying, no longer frightens him, and even does the complete opposite – brings him pleasure. We call this desensitisation and counter conditioning. We shape a dog's behaviour by breaking it down into manageable steps, and reward the dog for making progress towards the finished product.

Let's say you have a dog who is fearful of going in the car – crouches low and puts on the brakes, tail between his legs every time you have to go on a journey. Instead of never putting him in the car again, start to introduce it in a pleasurable way. Depending on the level of fear, perhaps start by just walking him around the car and dropping treats, then retreat to the house. Repeat for a few days. Step two –

and only ever move onto the next step once he is perfectly comfortable with the one before – open and close a door to the car, or the boot. The car is now moving and making a noise. Continue to drop treats around the car for him to sniff out. Then retire to the house again. After a few more days of that, or whenever he is ready, move on to step 3. Walk him up to the car, which by now should not signal that you will automatically put him in it, open the door and pop him in with his food bowl in front of him. Continue to feed in the car for a few days. Then step 4, feed in the car but this time turn the engine on. But don't go anywhere. Step 5, drive a few yards and back. Step 6, drive around the block. Still treating, etc, etc. Soon your dog should be looking forward to car journeys.

The same approach can be used for dealing with a dog who is scared of fireworks. Training needs to begin months before Guy Fawkes night or New Year's Eve. Pull up fireworks on your computer and turn the volume way down. If you have a balanced dog who won't react (or a deaf one), bring them along, for the fearful dog will be learning from them. Sit calmly and quietly – almost look bored, maybe yawn a little. Treat the dog with something it finds pleasurable: a toy, a treat, a massage. If he shows no reaction, turn up the volume a little, and continue with his pleasurable activity. We want the fireworks to represent relaxation, so when the big day comes, he will just curl up and go to sleep. If you have no time to prepare, and the day is upon you, turn up some soothing music to drown out the fireworks and act nonchalant. One behaviourist friend says she finds reggae music does the trick particularly well, especially if she gets the family singing and dancing to it as well. If the dog can see you are not bothered, he should see no reason to be bothered. You can also try a body wrap, which is a bit like swaddling a baby – it makes them feel safe. The worst you can do is feel sorry for your dog. He will sense it, and think there's something to worry about. And if he is shaking and nothing is working, DO NOT STROKE HIM. You will just have to respectfully leave him to work through this one on his own, and let him go wherever he feels safest.

Rocky during a firework display.
I fashioned a body wrap out of a woolly scarf.

When a dog is under stress, he will not sniff or pee or poo or eat. Not even the tastiest livercake will entice him. His bodily functions shut down. I would advise against trying to give treats to an anxious dog. By offering treats at a time of fear, you are actually rewarding the dog for being afraid. Instead, divert his attention onto something else. Walk him away and get him to give you eye contact – then by all means reward that.

The reason dogs will not eat when afraid is much the same as humans. Cortisol levels soar in preparation for fight or flight, and the digestive system shuts down to save energy. If the dog is unable to get away from the stimulus that is causing him stress, or if there is not sufficient time to recover between one stressful encounter and the next, the body will become exhausted. Prolonged periods of stress are likely to result in physiological and psychological damage, including high blood pressure, stomach ulcers, frequent urination, mood change and readiness for aggression, or learned helplessness (which is when the dog is too afraid to even move). He has come to believe that he cannot change the situation, so he gives up trying, even when opportunities for change become available. It is the most crippling and upsetting condition, and I am glad to say, I have not yet witnessed it first-hand.

Fearful dogs need the familiarity of a routine. It makes them feel safe. They should not be exposed to too many new stimuli at once. Rehabilitating a fearful dog takes time. Sometimes you have to take a huge step back, and make their world smaller, before you can take a step forward. They need the familiarity of the same people in the same surroundings with nothing unexpected happening to put them off balance. Once they have decompressed and are happy in their secure small world, you can gradually augment their world and introduce new stimuli.

Confidence levels of fearful dogs tend to be low, so I like to introduce challenges and games that they will succeed at, during their rehabilitation, in order to boost their self-assuredness. Take a look at chapter 22 on mental stimulation for ideas of games you can play with your dog. Always start easy. Never let him fail or get bored or confused, and always end on a high/success.

Case Study

I was called to the aid of an elderly couple in central London. They had a year-old English bull terrier called Geronimo who was petrified of life outside his apartment. I expected to see a sweet shy boy, so I was surprised to be greeted by an exuberant and happy chap who jumped all over me and was very over-excited to see me. I put my bag on the floor like I usually do when meeting dogs for the first time, as I like to assert myself from the off if they put their head inside to sniff around for the treats hiding at the bottom. I make the dog move away from the bag. The bag does not move away from the dog. Not so on this occasion. Geronimo picked the bag up in his mouth and ran around the apartment with it spraying its contents as he went.

"Gosh, he's a live wire, isn't he? When did he last go out?"

"Not for a few weeks, darling. It's too stressful for him, and I'm not strong enough to hold him."

I looked around the sumptuous apartment, laden with expensive antiques, to see the incongruous sight of pee pads strewn at intervals around the floor. There was no outside space, so Geronimo used the pads, but it was a bit hit and miss, so wherever he had peed in the past, they laid down another pad.

I had to get this boy out to see what all the fuss was about. I asked the owners to stay behind, in case they were fuelling his fear. He trotted down the stairs nicely beside me and into the entrance hall, then promptly slammed on the brakes as I opened the door to the street. He was strong, and there was

Common Problems and How to Fix Them

no way I could pull him from a standstill. I had to drain some of his pent-up energy. It's almost impossible to work with a dog who is wired up like a coiled spring. I used the stairwell as my training ground. Up and down we went, until I was too exhausted to run any more. I threw a ball down for him to chase, silently hoping that no elderly resident would be taking the stair option on the way up. Then I progressed to the entrance hall, and propped open the door so all his senses could take in the outside world. Then we continued with the ball games and chasing and treats, edging ever closer to the door. I threw the ball towards the door one final time, picked up the end of the lead he had been trailing, and ran with him to get the ball, but this time I used the momentum to carry on out of the door. With much praise and enthusiasm, I just kept walking. I didn't want to let his brain stop and think about what he normally did out here. He was doing OK until we hit roadworks one block from his front door. It's amazing how much louder they become when you listen from a dog's perspective. And then a car honked its horn and a lorry drove past splashing through a nearby puddle, which was one trigger too many for him, and he stopped abruptly. He wasn't shaking-in-his-boots afraid, but the tail was well between his legs and he started to stress pant. Although I couldn't persuade him to go any further (and I didn't want to put him through any additional stress anyway) he was more than happy to turn around and pull me all the way back to his apartment block. I had seen what I needed to see. Once inside, he gave a massive shake off, marched up the stairs, all relaxed again, and did a massive poo on the cream carpet outside his apartment. I mean, who puts a cream carpet in a communal hallway?

Unperturbed by the mess, his owner was actually impressed – amazed I had got him to the corner of the block, so I didn't feel like a complete failure. I was desperate to get this dog to a park, so he could run free, burn off energy and have a good sniff around. But living in Mayfair would mean walking through a minefield of his triggers for ten minutes before reaching a park. He was not ready for that. And besides, I wanted to remove him from the area he now associated with his fears. Geronimo had made a prisoner of himself, and had cut off any chance of socialisation with other dogs. I was convinced that if he walked in a pack, he would learn so much quicker to overcome his fears.

Since his owners did not have a car in London, and nor did they have the strength to walk Geronimo for the length he needed, I suggested two things. One, use taxis to get him to the park and back, and two, hire a dog walker. Luckily for Geronimo, money was no object when it came to providing for him, so his owners were only too happy to comply.

Geronimo's first trip to the park was memorable. I was there with my two dogs, having picked up Geronimo by car, and driven outside the city centre. He sniffed the air from the back of the car. A great sign that he was engaging with this new environment and not shutting down. I normally don't allow my dogs to jump straight out of the car as soon as the door is opened, but I encouraged it on this occasion, as I wanted to drum up some excitement for Geronimo. Seeing them bound out, he just followed. He was motionless for a moment, low to the ground as if trying to hold on tight, but when we all just walked off, throwing his favourite ball, he decided that was a better option. It was a joy to see him sniffing and trotting along behind.

Over the following six months, Geronimo was taken out almost every day to a park where he either had a short walk with his owners, or a longer one with a dog walker and a pack of dogs. He was so delighted to be in the company of other dogs that he soon forgot about the background noises of the city. Once he had formed a bond with a couple of the regular dogs, I suggested the dog walker take them along the pavement outside the park, but flanking it. Every week they were to include an extra little loop outside the park. Because neither dog walker nor dogs reacted to any of their surroundings, neither did Geronimo. Once he was comfortable walking outside the park, I suggested the taxi drop them off a block from the apartment, on the way home. This way, Geronimo would be in the territory he related with being the most fearful, but he would be heading home, which put him in a better frame of mind to cope with it, and having drained energy from the walk, he would be calmer. This worked a treat, and gradually they were dropped off further and further from the apartment, paying attention that Geronimo wasn't pushed over his threshold. He continues to do well, but not without the odd wobble when something catches him off guard. But I have taught his owners not to pander to him or feel sorry for him, and just adopt the 'don't be daft, let's go' approach.

CHAPTER 14
Aggression

The most serious problem by far is aggression: aggression towards another dog, and the pinnacle of unwanted dog behaviours, aggression towards people. As descendants from the wolf, all dogs still have a natural predatory urge. In the wild, wolves will do anything to not get injured. Getting injured is risky business – as a consequence, they may not be able to hunt, and subsequently they would starve to death. Picking a fight with another wolf therefore is a last resort, and most of the time those fights are for show and bravado, with a lot of growling and snapping of teeth, and not many actual wounds being inflicted. It is the same for domesticated dogs. They will do everything in their arsenal to first deflect a fight, before settling on dog-to-dog combat. One dog might simply diffuse a situation by ignoring another dog's antagonism, by turning his head, or walking away, for example.

If one dog is provoked by another, he will generally give a warning first. Let's say a young over enthusiastic adolescent cockapoo goes bounding up to an older Staffie cross, and jumps on him in an attempt to get him to play, but the Staffie wants to be left alone. The Staffie might go stiff and give a hard stare, or a lip curl, with a showing of teeth. If this is ignored, then he might escalate to a growl; if the growl is ignored, and the cockapoo is still in his face pestering him, and not getting the message, the Staffie might bite the air, and if that too isn't heeded, only then might he bite with intent to harm. Plenty of warning signs are usually given before an attack ensues. More often than not, the biter will get the rap. Especially if he's a Staffie cross. This cockapoo failed to heed the warning, and his owner failed to see that his 'playful' puppy was the one at fault. Lack of owner awareness is a major contributor to dog aggression. Now if the owner of the cockapoo had stepped in, and pulled his dog away, or if the owner of the Staffie had asked the owner of the cockapoo to take him away, they would have saved themselves a fight, and probably a lawsuit. But now, the cockapoo has learnt to fear all Staffies and the Staffie has learnt to be on his guard to defend himself against annoying puppies, because he can't rely on his owner to protect him.

Generally speaking, dogs don't cause fights. People do. Let me give another example. This one isn't caused by lack of human intervention, but intervention at the wrong time: we are walking down the street head on to another dog coming our way. Our dog looks up, interested by the other dog. We sense there might be a confrontation because the other dog looks scary to us. So we tense up and pull on the lead. We think we're keeping our dog close to us and out of harm's way. The dog thinks, "This must be a threat coming towards us, as my owner has gone all tense. He is in no state to take control of the situation, because he seems a bit afraid to me, so I'd better step in to protect us both". If he was off lead, he would probably choose to take a wide berth. But on a short lead he is forced to walk right up to the threat. What's more, we then pull back tighter on the lead, the closer we approach, raising the dog's head and shoulders, and actually putting him in an aggressive stance. The dog coming towards us sees this as a challenge, but he can't avoid the situation either, as he too is on a lead, and the only choice he has left is to defend himself by fighting. Then as the dogs engage, growling, we add fuel to the fire by shrieking and getting in a panic, and trying to get our hands in the way. This only serves to encourage and add excitement to the battle. Then we tear them apart, probably getting injured ourselves, and haul them away. Being immediately removed from the situation only serves to confirm to the dog that indeed the other dog was a real threat, a danger that must be kept away and he must be on his guard next time. Neither dog gets to calm down in the face of his nemesis, and realise he's not so bad after all, so a vicious circle is continued, and the behaviour gets worse and worse.

Other contributing factors to dog-on-dog aggression are:

- Barriers – a dog behind a door/fence will just want to get to the other side, to be with the 'free' dogs and people.
- Frustration. For example, being on a lead and not being allowed to interact with any other dog.
- Lack of human attention/intervention.
- Presence of high value food or toys.
- Head on meetings where dogs cannot move aside – pavements, corridors, entrances and exits.
- Poor breeding.

- Poor socialisation early on – leads to lack of confidence and fear.
- Over-confident risk-taking behaviour.
- Lack of trust in owner.
- Humans in an aroused state – running, screaming kids, arguing couples.
- Large numbers of dogs running together.
- Humans standing still – this encourages dogs to gather round them, and a stationary resource is easier to guard than a moving one.
- Arrival of aroused dogs in an uncontrolled state such as in a dog walker van.

The last three points are why dog parks are a hotbed for dog attacks. I'm not a fan of daycare either, because similar to dog parks, the dogs are milling around doing their own thing, with no calming breaks and no direction. Better to get yourself a dog walker (who doesn't go to dog enclosures). The dog will then be in following mode.

Dog-to-person aggression is as serious as behavioural problems get. Especially if that person is a child. I sympathise with anyone in this camp. You can live day-to-day on a knife edge, with your heart in your mouth most of the time, and it is very draining and distressing. I've been there.

More often than not, aggression towards humans is born of fear. It is a self defence mechanism which kicks in when the dog sees physical conflict as his only option: I'll attack you before you attack me. It can be learnt in puppyhood. The following scenario is typical of many first-time puppy owners. They are desperate to show off their new play thing, so invite friends and family round, without thinking about the welfare of the puppy, and his need to settle in slowly. The friends pick up the puppy, even if he is walking away, signifying he'd like space from the grabbing hands. Or maybe the puppy is seeking refuge behind its owner's legs. Someone approaches, and the owner moves his legs aside to allow the person to pick up the puppy. This only needs to happen a few times for the puppy to learn that walking away or seeking help don't work to secure peace and quiet. His next course of action may be to nip at the unwanted hands coming in to grab him. A puppy's nip does not deter most people from continuing to handle the pup. After all, it's what puppies do, and they're only playing, right? Continued exposure of this sort may lead the growing puppy to resort to a faster and stronger reaction next time: a growl and a bark as the stranger enters the room might work, and if that still doesn't deter them, then a stronger bite might do the trick. Before we know it, we have created a fear aggressive dog.

It's vital that we recognise when our puppy/dog has had enough of a situation. Just like humans, they need time out. The puppy's need (to be left alone) should come before our need (to play with/pet/ pick up the puppy). My puppy loves to come up onto the sofa for a cuddle. It's a wonderful feeling to have her curled up on my lap. After a minute or two, she always moves to the other end of the sofa or jumps down. I let her do just this, and do not grab her back, or go and sit with her on the floor. She is signalling she has had enough physical contact, and I respect that.

You *can* rehabilitate a dog who has learnt aggression as a response to fear, but it is a long process. The dog has to learn to trust you again.

A dog which has been physically abused, often street dogs (and some rescue dogs), are harder to rehabilitate because their aggression has become engrained and forms part of what they have learnt they need to do to survive. I shudder to think what must have happened to my Romanian rescue, to make him lunge at anyone with a raised arm or a stick or kicking a ball. He is not a bad dog. In fact, those he has nipped do not see him as a bad dog either, for my first job is to tell his story and get them to feel some compassion for him. It takes a great deal of time and patience and consistency to get the trust of a dog like this. It is trust that will cure him. Trust that you will keep him safe.

This trust is formed by connecting with your dog. Ask for eye contact often, and reward that eye contact. Play games that the dog enjoys. Always remain calm, and never raise your voice. Have a set of rules the dog has to abide by, and be consistent in keeping those rules. Keep unwanted attention away from him.

It is well documented that punitive methods can lead to making a behavioural problem worse, and this goes for aggression too. By punitive methods I mean use of a shock collar, use of a prong collar (popular in the States), hitting your dog, shouting at your dog. Even the use of some of the seemingly less harmful correction sprays can actually exacerbate a behaviour. Positive reinforcement methods are proven to have a better success rate at changing problem behaviours. As I mentioned in the introduction to Part 2, a little negative reinforcement (not punishment), in the form of a tweak on the lead, a touch to the rear, or a firm "No", can be beneficial to get the message across, of what is unacceptable behaviour, when used in conjunction with positive reinforcement. Of course the level of corrections used will vary tremendously from dog to dog, depending on their particular history.

First steps to take, before your appointment with the behaviourist, when you know you have an aggressive dog on your hands:

1. Invest in a muzzle. Introduce it slowly and positively. By this I mean, leave it lying around, so it becomes a familiar object. Then put a treat at the end of it and get your dog to put his nose in to retrieve the treat. Then take the muzzle away. Repeat a few times. And repeat for a few days. Now you are ready to fasten the muzzle for a few seconds after his nose has gone in for the treat. Then remove. Build the amount of time you leave it fastened. Now the muzzle has positive association, he should be happy wearing it. When you remove the muzzle at the end of prolonged wearing, you'll probably find that your dog gives a massive shake off, as he goes from a 'controlled' mindset to a 'released' one.
2. Keep your dog on a lead. Switch between short and long lead as the environment allows. He can still get plenty of exercise on a long lead, but you will have control if you need to rein him in.
3. Avoid situations you know will trigger him. Every time he acts aggressively towards another dog or person, that negative neural pathway gets stronger, so as much as possible, do not let him practise hostile behaviour.

The above points may prevent your dog attacking, but they won't change his overall mindset. This is where the behaviourist comes in. The behaviourist will approach the problem from the dog's psychological viewpoint. He or she will aim to create a new positive neural pathway, in place of the negative one. They will get the dog to think, "I see a dog I think might be a threat, but instead of attacking, I trust my owner to keep me safe, so I'll look up at her for reassurance first. She always gives me a treat when I look up at her, so I must be doing the right thing. And nothing bad ever happens. In fact, I don't mind other dogs now".

The same technique can be used, whether it's for dogs showing aggression to other dogs, people, bicycles, joggers, kids on scooters, cars etc. As I mentioned previously, work on a bond of trust, and secure some house rules first. Then arm yourself with a clicker and some high value treats, and set up some controlled meetings with your dog on a short lead. It would be normal at this point for a behaviourist to bring a control dog to the session, if there was a dog-on-dog problem. The control dog would be a very balanced and calm, probably older dog, who would not react in the face of a reactive dog. I take my 14 year old Labrador, Willa, but she should really be in retirement, so I have invested in a stuffed toy dog (or stuffie, as we call them), which seems to do the job just as well. I'll explain how to go about the rehabilitation, by using one of my most recent aggression cases as an example.

Case Study

Hope is a 1-year-old Staffie cross, rescued from Poland. Her previous owner kept her tied up all day (she has a scar round her neck to prove it). She was not socialised with other dogs. In fact, she was often in the presence of other dogs, but never allowed to get close to them, smell them or play with them. I imagine some of the scarring was from her pulling on the chain in a desperate bid to reach them. Like many of the bull breeds, Staffordshire bull terriers were originally bred for fighting, and were trained to be fearless and ignore pain. For this reason, Hope would probably not respond well to lead corrections. I was going to rely more on positive reinforcement to turn her around, and just use a vocal "No" correction if needed.

Hope's owner is a young Polish lady, 100% dedicated to her dog's rehabilitation. It is down to her that progress has been so positive and steady. I took the 'stuffie' along to the first session to see the extent of Hope's aggression. We introduced the dogs, on leads, from a distance, in the owner's garden. Completely fooled, Hope was beside herself with eagerness to get to the fake dog. I did not allow her to go bounding up. She was only allowed to approach a few paces closer once she had looked up at me and stopped pulling on the lead. Hope's owner had been doing some clicker training with Hope, so we continued with this to mark the positive behaviour. When Hope pulled on the lead towards the stuffie, I asked for her attention on me. As soon as her eyes locked with mine, I clicked and then took my time (to keep her attention on me longer) getting a piece of chicken out of my pouch. Then I threw it on the ground for her to sniff out. The longer I could distract her from the stuffie, the better, hence not just giving her the treat by hand.

We edged closer in this fashion until we reached the stuffie in a relatively calm state of mind. Calm is essential for a reactive dog meeting new dogs. I allowed Hope to sniff the stuffie, making sure the lead was slack, so as not to create any tension. She went for the tail area first and then the undercarriage. I could see her mouth start to quiver as she was literally sucking in the smell to 'taste' it with the Jacobson's organ in the roof of her mouth. Stimulated, she very quickly put her paws on the stuffie's back and started to growl and attempt to pin the stuffie to the floor. I pulled her away at this point as I had seen the level of her reactivity – which was pretty high. Rather than diving full-on into aggression, she got very over excited in such close proximity, and coupled with the smells (I had rubbed the toy against my own dog beforehand), led to her excitement boiling over into aggression. Deprived for so long, and unversed in the correct way to meet another dog, she was unable to contain herself. And all this over a stuffed toy. We had a long way to go.

I decided that repeated short sessions were necessary. I wanted Hope to eventually get used to the stuffie to the point of boredom. In fact, after three sessions, I was ready to take Willa with me. We introduced the dogs either side of a slatted fence. This way, Hope could see and smell her, but not harm her. The introduction was gradual as before, and at every step closer, Hope and I played another game or I asked for another command, to maintain her concentration, and keep her focus on me. I wanted to be more interesting to Hope, more fun and more rewarding than my dear Willa, which wasn't hard, as she played her part brilliantly, and turned away from Hope in complete avoidance. Willa is a very good judge of character and will always ignore or walk away when she senses unhealthy energy.

After a couple more sessions, Hope was able to sit a few feet from Willa (the same side of the fence) and ignore her, as us owners chatted. It was remarkable progress. Hope's owner and I swapped roles as she got Hope to focus on her, and I stood holding Willa. Movement usually brings about renewed intent, so the next challenge was to walk Willa away. Sure enough, Hope made a lunge for her, but her owner called her back, and she listened and obeyed and turned around. That was a hugely rewarding moment. It's always important to end a session on success, so we stopped there. The last thought Hope would be left with, was turning to her owner and getting praise and a treat.

The next steps were to leave the confines of the garden and go for a walk in parallel, but a few metres apart. When dogs walk together, pack mentality kicks in, and they walk as one. There were so many other distractions out on the street, that Hope barely noticed Willa trotting along beside her. She did pull towards a few other dogs we saw across the street, but she showed no more interest in using this behaviour towards Willa. Progress again.

The following week I borrowed a dog from a friend to introduce to Hope. The dog was an older intact male dachshund called Shreddie, who I hoped she would naturally respect. We met by a small park, chosen for its lack of dog walkers. The introduction took place either side of the fence, for protection, in case it all kicked off. Despite the owner's attempts to keep Hope's attention on her, Hope lunged at Shreddie. Shreddie put her in her place beautifully with a warning snap. She was learning that this was a disrespectful way to meet an older gentleman.

By the end of the session Hope was able to ignore Shreddie in favour of a ball. Again, we ended on success, creating more positive neural pathways in her brain.

Over the next few weeks, I introduced Hope to a few more dogs, in a controlled way, and gradually built up her repertoire of successful meetings. Four months later Hope's owner called to tell me she was now able to walk Hope off lead, in a small pack, with no issues. A remarkable turnaround in such a short space of time. It has taken time, patience and dedication, but I am lucky that she had that in spades.

Hope and her owner in front of the stuffie.

Huge progress on one of our later sessions, when I introduced Hope to two well balanced dogs. Notice how the other dogs are intentionally ignoring her, turned away. They do not wish to engage in her unstable energy and she is not fixated on them either.

The majority of aggression cases I see are fear based. Cases like the one cited above are overstimulation and excitement based. Just occasionally I get a case where the aggression is 'pleasure' based. This is when the dog is actually getting a high from attacking another dog. It makes him feel good or powerful that he has made another dog move away by attacking it. These are more serious cases, as the problem is harder to eradicate. If the dog is getting a dopamine hit every time he goes on the attack, then the way to overcome it is to offer something that will provide a better dopamine hit. It might be a squeaky ball or a really high value treat. That's the positive reinforcement. For the dog who finds attacking fun, then the fun must be taken out of it. There must be a consequence for his actions. A firm "No", a tug and

Common Problems and How to Fix Them

release on the lead, a touch correction. That's the negative reinforcement.

I am seeing a particularly feisty young border terrier at the moment called Betsy, who likes to go for puppies. I'm sure it started as a warning defence mechanism towards puppies who got too close. After all, puppies can be very annoying. But after a while, she began to seek them out, and actually go bolting from one side of the park to the other in order to hunt one down. She saw them as defenceless prey, and it became quite a fun game, which made her feel good. Border terriers are ratters by nature and it's in their breeding to hunt down and kill small rodents, badgers and foxes. Betsy was acting to type. Also, having reached 1 year of age, she was no longer the new kid on the block, and with the surge of hormones that comes at adolescence, she found a new confidence which allowed her to boss around the younger ones. I also think her owner's actions had been fuelling these fights: the anxiety, the nervous high-pitched calling of "Betsy, Betsy" over and over, and the lack of enough rules to keep Betsy in check. We have done several sessions together, and she is now a master of the 'eye contact, click and reward sequence'. Betsy is a glutton for chicken, so that is to our advantage. If she looks at a puppy, then looks up at her owner, she gets a click and piece of chicken for making the right decision, and then they move on. Betsy no longer hightails it across the park to her next 'victim'. She only reacts if puppies come into her face space, so we are now working on getting her to ignore that for chicken too. Easy when the meetings are controlled and the puppy is on a lead. Not so easy when you are in a central London park during lockdown, which is teeming with puppies off lead. Progress is slow, and when Betsy does react, she gets a firm

"No" and a follow through with eye contact. If her reaction is intense, I give a firm tug on the lead. I then make her stay in front of her 'victim' until she is calm. I don't want her to get a kick out of sending another dog packing. Betsy's owner has to continually find new ways to be the most fun thing in the park. She must be the drug of choice.

And here's a final word on aggression: if you ever approach another dog and you hear their owner saying to them "Be nice" – run for the hills!

CHAPTER 15
Resource Guarding

When a dog is overly possessive towards an item he covets (and this can include food, a toy, the house, another dog, or a person), it is called resource guarding. In the wild, guarding valuable resources such as a water hole or a fresh kill, is a matter of life or death, so it's no wonder that this trait has been passed down to our domesticated dogs. Some dogs have more of an inclination towards it than others, and this is not just down to nature, but also nurture. A lack of rules and boundaries and allowing your dog the run of the entire house, can lead to him thinking the house and furniture belong to him. If you have ever approached your sofa where your dog is lounging, and he has growled at you, then you may be able to relate to this. He is guarding it. Top dogs always take the best sleeping spot.

It may not be news to you, having read this far, but it is YOU who should be top dog. I don't mean this in a dominating way, but in a guiding, trusting, assertive way. If my dog growled from his place on my sofa, I would immediately say "Off", and gently push his rear so that he removed himself. Then I would sit firmly down in his spot, so claiming it back for myself. Then I would make all furniture out of bounds for him, never allowing him to settle on any again, unless at my invitation. I would not, however, advise anyone to adopt this approach without the help of a behaviourist. Confronting a growling dog could be asking for trouble. This is why it's important to enforce boundaries from the start; so avoiding this predicament altogether.

Some dogs like to lounge in doorways, at the bottom of the stairs or by the front door. If they have no behavioural issues, I see no need to move them. They have realised that this is where the action happens – the comings and goings they don't want to miss out on. However, if your dog takes umbrage every time someone (and this can be a household member or a visitor) crosses his path, this must be addressed. It should not be his job to decide who can or can't enter, and who leaves. In no uncertain terms I would say "Move", and walk towards him. Usher him to his bed in another room. If he is moved on every time he lies by the front door, he will eventually just get up and move away at the mere sight of you approaching.

Be wary about letting your dog win at tug of war, or chasing him around when he has stolen your slipper. It can inadvertently encourage guarding. If he takes the slipper to his bed, and puts a paw on it, he is further claiming it, and any approach at this stage would probably elicit a growl. If you enter into a fight over the slipper, you will be teaching him to guard it better next time – maybe with bite. If however, you walk past him with the smell of delicious treats in your hand, or his favourite toy, and throw them away from his bed, likelihood is that he will leave the slipper to go and fetch the higher value prize. This way, there is no confrontation, and he has learnt that a human approaching his bed is good stuff. But be aware of your timing of the treat giving – you don't want him to start associating stealing your slipper with getting a reward. So don't react the second he grabs the slipper if you can help it. Act all nonchalant. Act like *you* have decided to start a new game, and that you are not reacting to him starting the game. Better still, teach him a 'drop' command. He should come to you with the slipper, drop it and then be rewarded.

Before any guarding issues develop, introduce 'drop'. As your dog/puppy is chewing on a toy, approach with a delicious treat and put it under his nose. As (and not before) he opens his mouth to take the treat, say 'drop' (or 'leave' or 'dead' – whatever you want to adopt). The toy will fall out as he opens his mouth for the treat. He will soon associate opening his mouth with the with the word 'drop'. Pick up the toy – do not snatch it away fast as this will encourage him to snatch it back. Then give the treat. Then give him *back* the toy. This is key. He has then learnt that he does not need to guard his toys because you will always give them back. Once practised several times over a few days, you can progress to saying 'drop' *before* he opens his mouth, as he will now know what this means.

If he later grabs an item you don't want him to have, put the treat under his nose, say "Drop", take away the item, and offer him another item he *can* have.

It's very tempting to immediately pounce on your new puppy who has picked up something that may be harmful to him. One day it could be a small item like a piece of plastic rubbish, another day a marble, another day some wire cables. All which might present a choking hazard. He is merely being curious, but he is learning that every time he finds something interesting, the human comes along and prizes his jaws apart and steals his find. Next time he will have to fight a bit harder if he wishes to retain his find. This is how humans create guarding issues.

It's vitally important from day one to puppy proof your house to prevent your pup grabbing things he shouldn't. Clear away anything you don't want him to chew. Put in baby gates to keep him out of rooms you want to preserve in their current state. To satisfy his curiosity of new objects and textures, give him plenty of objects he can investigate. These could include carboard boxes, old socks knotted in the middle, old bits of hosepipe, old magazines, egg boxes, old tea towels, toilet rolls etc, etc. My pup played with a single blueberry for about ten minutes straight, such was her curiosity of the smell, taste, texture, size. Leave these objects lying around, and don't snatch them away when your puppy goes in for a sniff or a chew. If he picks up one of the items and runs off, do not chase him. If he brings an item to you, gently stroke him while he has it in his mouth. Show him there is no competition for items. If he does manage to grab one of your favourite cushions, walk *away* from him and go and get an item he *can* play with, then animate the item – wiggle it around or throw it across the room. I'd be very surprised if he didn't drop the cushion to go and chase the permitted item.

Amongst themselves, dogs sort out disputes over possessions fairly quickly, and often without any fight. One dog might simply stand over another who is in his sleeping spot, until the weaker one simply gets up and moves away. In the same way, I try and solve some guarding issues by being more like a dog. For example, I was boarding a Pomeranian for a few days, to tackle his guarding issues. I thought that if I started work on him out of his own territory, I would have more success. In his own home he had been guarding his crate, the family sofa and a younger dog in the house. None of the family members could approach any of these things without the Pom growling at them. So new house, new boss, new rules. Day one, he jumped onto the sofa, and I told him to get off in a calm but firm manner. He didn't try and get up again. Day two, he felt a little more settled, and as I walked past his crate when he was resting there after supper, he growled. He was basically saying, "Keep away from my turf". Rather than reach a hand into the crate to remove him, and risk a bite, I closed the crate door and sat down next to the crate. I was saying (without uttering a word), "It's my house and I'll go where I want". He growled and lunged at me in protest. Even though my supper was boiling over on the stove, I could not get up and move away to rescue it, as the Pom would perceive that it was his growling that had been successful, and made me move away. He continued to growl and lunge, and of course I felt perfectly safe as he was behind bars, so I continued to sit calmly. He was expending a lot of energy growling. Sooner or later, he would run out of steam and would have to give it up. Surrender. That was all I was asking. I turned to face him and meet his gaze, which was a direct confrontation. After ten minutes of continuous growling and air snapping, he lay down panting, but still growling. After a further ten minutes he was quiet, but exhausted, and no longer interested in me. I opened the crate door, he walked out and he allowed me to stroke him. He had surrendered, my supper was ruined, but I had claimed my territory back. No grudges held on either side.

The Pomeranian guarding
his crate from me.

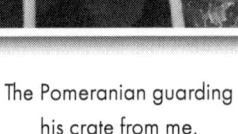

All smiles
afterwards.

A common problem I get asked about is food guarding. I recently had dinner with a girlfriend, and as normally happens, the conversation soon turned to dogs. She was baffled that her dog had food guarding issues, since she had trained him against it. "How did you train him?" was my first question. Inevitably I discovered that she had actually trained her dog to *become* a food guarder. She would take away the dog's bowl several times while he was eating, to show the dog, so she thought, that the bowl belonged to her. She also wanted the dog to get used to someone approaching his bowl, as they were having a baby and didn't want the dog to feel that a baby crawling around his food bowl was a threat. If I was that dog, I would have been mighty disgruntled at having my food taken away from me, not just once during a meal time, but two, three or four times. The first few meal times I might let it slide, but if this became a habit, I would become increasingly annoyed, and probably give a warning growl. This sort of behaviour is akin to malicious teasing after all. If my meal was still interrupted, even after this warning, I would probably increase the intensity of my growl, showing more teeth or even biting. What my friend had not realised either, was that by giving the food bowl back to her dog while he was still growling, she was rewarding the growl and thus encouraging it. Yet again, another classic case of 'misguided owner', not 'bad dog'.

To undo what she had created, I suggested the following: next meal time she was to put the food bowl down with only a small handful of the dog's usual kibble in it. As the dog was eating, she should bend down with another handful of kibble and throw it into the bowl. She was to continue in this way until the dog had eaten the whole meal. Her dog would then soon learn that a hand approaching his food bowl meant a positive thing – more food – and he would soon learn to welcome it. She was to repeat this process for a few days. Then she could revert to giving her dog all its food in the bowl at once, but this time, as the dog was eating, she should approach the bowl and toss in some high value pieces of food, like cooked meat. If she continued with this behaviour every so often, her dog would be only too happy to allow her or a toddler near his coveted bowl of food.

Case Study 1

I encountered a particularly nasty case of food aggression within my first few months of qualifying. I was not confident enough to command a proper fee (due to lack of experience), but the advantage of this was that I could help people who might not otherwise be in a position to get support. I drove to a council estate in north London, where I was met by a woman and her black Labrador in a tiny one-room bedsit. Room and owner matched in unkemptness, but the dog was a handsome fellow, and she had obviously looked after him well. He was an intact one-year-old and very friendly, greeting me with a waggly bum and an energetic bounce. Owner and I chatted for a while, and her Lab seemed the perfect companion. He came and sidled over to me and asked for some affection. He gave lovely soft eye contact and sat beautifully on command when I offered a treat. It was hard to imagine that he was anything other than your usual soppy, friendly, easy-going Labrador.

I asked her to show me the usual feeding time ritual. She jumped up with a chipper, "Come on Banjo, supper time!" He then followed her at her heels to the small galley kitchen, where she prepared his food, allowing him a few barks and jumps. Then she virtually threw the bowl down at him and ran back. "Look what happens now", she said. She took a step towards him and immediately Banjo revealed his other side. He started to growl and bare his teeth as he scoffed his food hurriedly, with legs splayed over the bowl and his gaze up at her. She took another small step towards him and he suddenly lunged forward lashing out at her, barking and growling, flashing a full display of the weapons in his mouth. Luckily, she was quick to dodge him. "Ok, ok, I get the picture," I quickly interjected. I was keen for her not to lose a limb on my watch. We let Banjo finish what was in his bowl, and I suggested a new method.

Banjo saw the bowl as his, and the flat as his, and his mistress as his. First we needed to set some boundaries to change this around. Even though the bedsit was basically only 2 rooms, I explained to the owner that she still had to claim some space for just herself. The bathroom would now be off limits to the dog, as would be the owner's bed. Banjo was also not to be allowed over the threshold to the kitchen while she prepared his food. There was to be no excitement. No heralding of mealtimes. She was just to get up calmly and go to the kitchen. If Banjo started being demanding, jumping and barking, she was to go and sit back down again. If he followed her into the galley, she was to walk into him to make him back up. Then she was to get him to stay behind the entrance while she prepared his food. Instead of putting the bowl on the floor, where he could easily guard it, she was to hold it. The bowl belonged to her now. She was to approach him, feed him by hand, one mouthful at a time, and he had to sit and give eye contact for every mouthful.

The meal went without incident. We were creating a little respect. She was never any threat to him, because approaching him meant she was coming with a reward, not coming to take away his prize. We had totally turned the meaning of approaching Banjo at mealtime on its head.

Since things were going well, I decided to up the stakes. I had seen a little video on YouTube I wanted to mimic, and this seemed like the perfect time. I tied Banjo to a door handle, just giving him enough lead to drop his head, but not so much that he could touch the floor with his nose. I produced from my rucksack the highest value of all treats – a raw bone. It was a fairly heavy knuckle bone, and purposefully big enough that he couldn't fit it all in his mouth. I gave him the bone, which he snatched and started to growl, threatened by my proximity. I remained quiet and did not back away. Now, because he could not lower his head to the floor, he was unable to get much purchase on the bone. He couldn't put a paw on it. Nor could he chew it because the moment he tried to, it fell out of his mouth and hit the floor where he was unable to reach it. I let him stare at it for a bit, then I picked it up and gave it back to him. This time he did not snatch it away. He soon figured out that he could only chew away on it if I was holding it. As he got stuck in, I released the bone and it fell to the floor. This time I backed away. Again he tried to pick it, again he failed. I approached him, reached for the bone again and gave it to him, holding on so he could chew away at it. Every time he got stuck in, I released my hold and backed away. The bone either fell straight to the floor, or he would hold it in his mouth until he had to release it. He started to look up at me 'asking' me to come and pick up the bone for him. After a few repetitions, and with no words at all from me, he had realised that getting the bone meant teamwork. He could not chew on it without my help. He willed me to approach him; he willed me to pick up the bone; he willed me to keep a hold of it as he ate it. Approaching him while there was a bone at his feet was welcomed. He was learning the benefits of sharing.

If I had told Banjo's owner an hour earlier that he would let my hand be on his prized bone as he ate it, she would not have believed me. And yet here he was. This was an excellent trust-building exercise, not to be attempted without Banjo being tied up. If he was able to take the bone away, or to his bed, there would be trouble. Nor was it an exercise to be repeated too often, as I suspect he might have become frustrated. But it was an excellent first step.

Case Study 2

I have a Romanian street dog, Rocky, who is very fearful. After he settled into the house, when he first came to us, his guarding tendencies began. Once he figured out he was here to stay, and this was his home, he felt the old default position kick in, and was ready to defend his home from anyone he felt threatened him.

Now, if I was my client, I would assume that the dog felt a need to take on being defender of the house, because the owners were not stepping up to the plate and making the dog feel safe. I knew full well, I had rules and boundaries in place and was certainly the boss and protector of my dog. So why should my dog feel the need to defend me/the house? Every stranger, especially men, who came to the house, would get met with vicious growling and barking. He would literally try and bite the door, before they even entered.

I put him on a lead for meeting new people at the door. This way he calmed down and accepted them. The fact was that he felt *I* was in charge of the situation. It was when he was left to his own devices that he panicked, and would revert to his fear aggressive tactics.

Once inside, guests relaxed and so did Rocky. However, if they got up to move, and I was not near them – for example if they went to the loo – Rocky would resume his fearful guarding and go for the bite. I'm afraid he nipped a few people who came to my house. Not a great advertisement for a behaviourist.

I called on the help of another behaviourist. She was a specialist in treating ex-street dogs. She explained that they take much longer to rehabilitate. Losing his shelter on the street would have been a matter of life or death for Rocky.

Goodness knows what experience he had had of men in the past, but clearly he had felt his life was threatened by them as well. He might never be comfortable with strangers in his house. The behaviourist suggested I 'take away' the front door from Rocky. It was to be none of his business who came and went. When the doorbell went, I was to lock him in another room, and let him out only once guests were seated and armed with treats. Then I would bring him out on a lead and introduce him to the guests, and encourage him to take treats from them.

In theory this sounded like a good plan, however, locking a barking dog behind a door, only serves to get him more wound up, in my experience, and wanting to be the other side of it. Predictably, Rocky did not respond well. If he wasn't to spend the rest of his life barking, locked behind a door in another room, or crated, I was going to have to find another way.

Since he was responsive when I was around, but unpredictable when making decisions on his own, I took the rather drastic measure of tethering him to me, whenever anyone came round, or even just rang the bell. This involved a short lead clipped to my waist, with Rocky within short distance of me. Every Amazon delivery man, every postman, every friend of my teenage kids, sparked him up. When they were at the door, I called Rocky to me, waited until he was calm, clipped him onto me and then opened the door. He then had to remain close to me until they had left. This was the only way I found successful in controlling the house guarding situation. He trusted me more than he trusted himself, and it continues to be an on-going daily challenge, just to keep him relaxed in his own home.

Common Problems and How to Fix Them

Rocky lunging at the men who came to read the meter. They are looking directly at him which will have escalated his attack, as this is very confrontational in dog language. Although he is tethered to me, I let him have a longer rein so I could prompt a reaction and film it.

CHAPTER 16
Copraphagia (poo eating)

As disgusting as this sounds, eating stool is a perfectly natural thing for a dog to do. A bitch with a litter of pups cleans up their mess by eating it. The pups in turn, having watched mum, might mimic this behaviour later on. However, the explanation is not always this simple. There may be several other reasons why your dog is eating his own or another dog's faeces.

1. If your dog has an intestinal problem, then he may not be digesting the nutrients in his food properly. If this is the case, the waste product that comes out the other end will be as high in nutrients as when it went in, according to the dog, so the clever thing to do would be to eat it. Always wise to get your dog checked over by a vet to rule this out first.
2. If you are feeding a low-grade kibble with poor protein content (less than 50%), your dog may not be getting all the nutrients he needs. His body will be telling him to make up for this deficiency

by eating more. Some modern day kibbles are packed with colourings and flavourings, to appeal to the human, and bulked out with soya and vegetables, most of which a dog's stomach cannot digest, so they get passed through the system and out the other end. The added preservatives make the stool smell particularly delicious to a dog – so why wouldn't he eat it? And it still tastes good because of all those indigestible flavourings. To him it's the same as walking past a sandwich which has been dropped on the floor. Madness! You wouldn't catch a dog eating the stool from a raw fed dog – it's pretty compact, as all nutrients are absorbed by the body, and mostly waste product such as bits of bone and cartilage come out the other end.

3. Check that you are feeding your dog enough. Underfed dogs will go to great lengths to stop themselves feeling hungry. It's a survival mechanism.

    Diabetes, Cushing's disease, thyroid disease, steroids and parasites can also cause an increase in your dog's appetite.

4. Excessive punishment can cause a dog to eat his stool. If he has pooed in the house while being toilet trained, or out of stress at being left on his own, and the owner returns to chastise him, he will soon learn that a poo on the floor coupled with his human's return, is bad news. He may eat the poo to eliminate the inevitable negative outcome. Clever, I say!

5. It may be an attention-seeking behaviour. If you have ever seen your dog sniffing a poo, and thought he might be about to eat it, you may react by shouting and running at him, arms flailing. If your dog is the confident type, and if you don't interact with him as much as you could, he may view this as the perfect time to get you running around after him in a fun game of chase. Once he has learnt this gets your attention, he may escalate to eating the poo, which seems to get an even greater reaction. In cases like these, you would do best to ignore the poo sniffing and eating, and add a distraction before he even gets the chance to sniff. Call him to you for a treat or throw a ball or engage him in another activity. Once you give your attention to him in positive ways, he won't need to attract your 'bad' attention by eating poo.
6. Dogs who are confined in a small space for long periods or who are kept in isolation, often show poo eating behaviour.

Clear up your garden regularly to eliminate the start of a bad habit.

Best of all, teach your dog a 'leave it' command, and then reward him with a really tasty treat. Tastier than poo.

CHAPTER 17
Inappropriate Toileting

Your dog is house trained. However, you still discover the odd accident inside, mostly on your bed. Or perhaps you take your dog for a long walk, where he 'does' nothing, yet as soon as he walks in the door, he wees on your carpet. Or maybe you just can't comprehend why he would wee in his food bowl?

There are several reasons why your dog could be peeing/pooing in the house:

1. Medical condition. He may have a urinary tract infection, incontinence (especially in older dogs), kidney disease, diabetes, intestinal parasites or some other health problem. Some medications can cause incontinence as well. Rule these out first, with a visit to the vet.
2. Fear. Dogs have been known to pee or even poo, when faced with a stressful or fearful event. Much like a human.
3. Excitement. For example, when you come home from work and make a huge fuss over the dog.

Ignore the dog (until he is calm) and the peeing will stop. Yeah, that's a hard one.
4. Marking. He's saying, "I own that".
5. Submission. They may be faced with another dog or person they see as intimidating. They pee to show they are no threat.
6. Overstimulation when on walks. No time to relax and sniff to do a pee/poo.
7. A previous pee/poo is not properly cleaned up, and the lingering smell stimulates the dog to go in those places.
8. Not quite house trained. Your dog is peeing in the back garden ok, but when on walks he holds it in, as this is fairly new territory and he hasn't learnt to relax out there yet. When he gets back home, he relaxes and goes to his familiar spot where he knows he'll get praised for it.
9. Out of desperation. If not let out frequently enough, they won't be able to hold it in any longer. Puppies obviously need to be let out much more frequently than adults. They can only hold their bladders for their age in months, ie, a 3-month-old pup can hold its bladder for 3 hours (in a crate). They need letting out every hour when not contained.

In none of the above cases should you scold the dog. Punishment is known to make the situation worse. In most cases, he won't know what he is being scolded for anyway, so he will be confused and feel threatened by your behaviour – which will lead to more pooing and peeing.

A recent client called me, explaining that her dog was pooing on her bed out of revenge for her being gone for long periods. I explained that dogs live in the moment and do not rationalise or think about the future or past. More than likely, the dog was stressed at being on its own for so long, and sought out a place of comfort – her bed, which smelt of her. The poo was probably just involuntary loss of sphincter control, brought on by stress.

But not all accidents on owners' beds are this sympathetic. More often than not, it's a result of a dog living with a lack of rules. He doesn't know you are the boss. He has intentionally put his smell over your smell, claiming the bed as his own. He might also have no regard for peeing elsewhere in the house. If he views the house as his, chances are, he may pee on it. Introduce some rules and make sure he respects them (see chapter 3).

Case Study

I had a FaceTime consultation with a client who lived too far away for me to see in person.

She had recently adopted a 6 year old female Westie. She already had a 2 year old male Westie, who I had seen a year earlier. She was concerned about the relationship between the two of them. The female had only been with them a week, and the male was showing his displeasure at the new arrival. He had moved her from her seated position a couple of times, by standing over her. She had growled at him a couple of times when he walked past her bed. She was fearful when outside, as she had never been walked or socialised. She had been used purely as a breeding machine. However, when walked with the male, Wilby, she seemed much happier.

It was inside that the issues happened, and usually over resources: her bed, his food, their owner. At first, I thought that Wilby was being bossy and jealous about sharing his mistress. He objected when his owner showed the new dog affection. In photos I had been sent, the female was always turned away from Wilby, in avoidance, and she didn't look particularly relaxed. I assumed Wilby was the one that needed addressing. It was only at the very end of our meeting that the owner mentioned the female's strange behaviour at the end of every meal. Once the food bowls had been taken away, she peed directly on the spot where Wilby's bowl had been. At first, the owner thought it was a lack of house training, but night after night, the peeing in the same spot told her otherwise.

The new dog was sending a clear message to Wilby, and claiming his eating area. This might have escalated to a fight if left unchecked. She seemed like the innocent party, but was actually the feisty one. Wilby had just been putting her in her place and telling her to respect the house rules. I told the owner to change up the scene. Although she had been supervising mealtimes, I advised feeding Wilby in a different spot and separating the dogs at feeding time. The female was not to see where he was fed, or see when the bowl was lifted. They were to be treated equally and any reason for giving the other competition, was to be taken away. We scheduled another meeting for a week's time, but never needed it, as the dogs became best of friends. Well, in my head they did – no, they just became tolerant of each other.

Common Problems and How to Fix Them

Wilby (foreground) and his new companion. This photo was sent to me by the owner when she first asked for help. Notice how the female rescue is not relaxed. Eyes are wide, ears pricked and she looks ready to move. Wilby is turned away from her, also with ears pricked. The photo told me these two are not friends.

CHAPTER 18
Excessive Barking

Dogs bark for various reasons: to alert their 'pack' that something unfamiliar is approaching; to get your attention; to keep a threat away; through excitement, distress, separation anxiety or boredom. Your dog is trying to communicate his feelings, and that is completely natural. However, excessive barking is an issue, not just because it's annoying to listen to, but because it means your dog is unbalanced. If this is your problem, ask yourself if all your dog's needs have been met. Has he been sufficiently walked to drain excessive energy? Is he constantly faced by something he perceives as a threat? Has he had any mental stimulation or is he bored and frustrated? Is he overstimulated, overexcited and unable to calm himself?

I always say 'a calm dog is a happy dog'. A calm dog is also more predisposed to being a healthy dog. No pressure on the heart and lungs, no excessive release of cortisol in readiness of fight or flight. Allow a dog to release its energy by walking it twice a day, and motivate it to work for its food, and stimulate it mentally; give it an outlet for its natural dog breed tendencies, and it should be too tired to even be bothered to bark.

Common Problems and How to Fix Them

Coupled with the walking, you also need to disagree with the barking. If you don't, how does the dog know it's not a behaviour you want? Not disagreeing with it, is allowing it. Try and catch the barking before your dog is in full flow. Once he has escalated, it is much harder to calm his brain down. Nip it in the bud – at the very first bark, calmly but firmly say "tshh" and take a step towards him, looking him in the eye. No frustration or shouting – that just adds fuel to the fire. Let your body posture and your energy do the work.

I have had several clients who have asked me in desperation, "But how do I stop him barking?" I quite simply reply, "Tell him not to". They get the hoover out, or whatever triggers him, to put me to the test, "Hey, tshh". And that's it. All quiet. One of my clients told me it's a bit like getting an electrician round to change a light bulb. Simple, and rather embarrassing.

If the barking stems from over excitement, be aware of your own behaviour. Likelihood is, your dog will be mirroring your mood. You may be a very busy, chatty or anxious type, always rushing around, with lots going on around you. Dogs get caught up in this energy. It's not very relaxing for them. If this is the case, be sure to give the dog periods of calm and time out. They should be able to relax in your presence too, so I don't mean just shutting them in another room on their own. You are in control of all your dog's emotions, so it's your job to instil the calm in the presence of what excites him.

Case Study

This is one of my more peculiar cases. I got a call from a very courteous young Chinese lad around 16 years old, asking for help for his one-year-old bichon frise called Yat-Yat. He lived together with his mother and grandmother in an apartment on the river in west London. It was the beginning of the first wave of Coronavirus. A few Londoners had begun to wear masks, but for the most part we were widely ignorant of the seriousness of the disease yet to take its grip on our country. Having arrived from Hong Kong just a few months earlier, my Chinese family were well aware of the risks, and hesitant about allowing a stranger into their home.

I arrived masked (first time ever) at their request. Yat-Yat (or Yap-Yap, as I called her) barked all day long. She barked at noises outside, she barked at her owners, she barked at me when I entered. Funnily enough, they didn't seem to mind the barking per se, it was the fear of complaints that prompted them to call me, because dogs were not allowed in this apartment block. If they got busted with a dog, they would be thrown out, and they had nowhere else to go. No family, no friends, and, so they told me, no money.

The first question I ask of an overly barking dog, is how much exercise it is getting, so I began, "How often do you take her out?"

"A few times a day", was the reply. So far, so good.

"And how long is each walk?"

"Huh?" They didn't seem to understand the question.

"Is she on or off lead for the walk?" I rephrased.

"There is no need for a lead on the balcony."

It transpired that they ushered the dog to the 3'x8' balcony a few times a day to do its business. The dog had not been outside the apartment all week.

Well, here was the source of all their problems. I

explained that dogs have a certain level of energy in a day that has to go somewhere. In the absence of any mental or physical exercise, Yat-Yat's energy was going into barking. She was bored and frustrated. She was not able to use her nose smelling all the offerings that the outdoor world has to offer. Even lap dogs need to be walked, I explained, and to follow a leader.

I immediately suggested an outing, and was met with consternation. The building had a 24-hour doorman, which meant that they could not walk the dog through the lobby and out the main door. Luckily, their apartment was on the ground floor, and on the few occasions the dog did leave the house, she had to be smuggled out of the bathroom window. So I found myself, standing in the flowerbed, ready to receive a ball of quivering fluff that was being lowered into my arms by the grandmother, who was standing inside, in the bath. I offered to take the dog on my own for the first walk so I could assess her properly. She seemed to be a constant wreck in the presence of her owners.

As her feet touched the ground, she did a massive shake off. (When a dog shakes as if it has been wet, it is actually shaking off a state of mind, and relaxing.) Without letting her think too much, I started to run. We ran and we ran. All along the riverside and looped back along the streets. She skipped, sniffed, said hello politely to other dogs. It was a joy to see such a different dog unfold so quickly. Not a single bark.

Once back outside the apartment, I encouraged the family to join me. They all needed to be on board if things were going to change, and I wanted them to learn how to walk Yat-Yat on a loose lead, with no tension. The mother appeared on the balcony, flustered, and the dog immediately started to bark. She was definitely feeding off the negative energy. Only the son came with me and showed a keenness to learn. He forthrightly explained that he could not expect to get the rest of the family on board. He was the only one who ever took the dog out and that was seldom, because he was either away at school, or when home, he had to study hard for some important exams. I queried that surely he couldn't study *all* day, and that having breaks and fresh air might actually improve his brain power. No, apparently breaks were not permitted.

After our training walk, and once smuggled back into the apartment (which was quite a feat, as the window was a full arm's length height above our heads), Yat-Yat seemed calmer. The grandmother immediately whisked her away to give her a bath. This, they explained, was because of all the germs she must have picked up outside. Not just a paw wash. A full top to toe shampoo bath. They were paranoid about the dog picking up the Coronavirus and infecting them.

Earlier they had been talking about how sensitive Yat-Yat was. She had many allergies and despite being on a special diet, she scratched herself permanently. There is little one can do in the face of such strong beliefs, but I did insinuate that all that washing was no doubt washing away the dog's natural protective oils, and replacing them with potential harmful and irritant chemicals.

That evening, the son texted me to thank me profusely for the session. Yat-Yat had been calm since I left. He assured me they would move house soon, so they could take her out more often and more easily.

Common Problems and How to Fix Them

Six months later I received another text from him. Yat-Yat had resumed the barking, and had escalated to growling at the three of them. Recently, she had bitten his mother. They desperately needed my help. I phoned and began with the same question as before.

"How often are you taking her out?"

"Well, we've been very busy, and I have been studying very hard, and what with lockdown and everything…"

"How often? Once every 3 days?"

"Well, to be honest, none of us have left the apartment for 2 months."

There is very little I can do, if a dog's basic needs are not met, and the owners do not follow my advice. Most dogs during lockdown were getting more walks, not fewer, as walking was one of the few activities left that were still legal. There was no excuse for this in my mind. Of course the dog was biting them – quite frankly, I felt like biting them! And it was only going to escalate. I candidly gave him three solutions:

1. Walk the dog (and move out of that apartment).
2. Pay a dog walker to walk the dog.
3. Give the dog up for adoption.

It's very sad really to be unable to help a dog, and to see a family living in such fear. That fear and negativity was fuelling the dog's anxieties, 24/7, with no break. I have never before suggested rehoming for any of my dog patients, but here it was clearly in the dog's best interests. I don't know what decision the family made. Sadly, I suspect, none of the above.

NO SUCH THING AS A BAD DOG

Yat-Yat being smuggled out of the bathroom window.

CHAPTER 19
Quirky Behaviour

I wasn't sure which chapter to put these anomalies into, so I have created one just for them.

I love a challenge, and every now and again something curious pops up, which draws me in, and forces me to put my detective hat on. Your dog may have his own peculiarities, and I would love to hear about them. Whatever the problem, the remedy is basically the same. Remain calm and assertive. Tell your dog not to do the 'thing'. Use some counter conditioning. Change *your* behaviour.

Case Study 1
When I was just starting out as a behaviourist and offering my services for free, I went to see a lady who lives on my street who has a Maltese. She demonstrated that every time she opened the freezer door, her dog ran off in fear to the room next door. The fridge door produced no such effects. Just the door above it. Clearly something had happened in relation to the freezer, to scare her pooch in such a way, but she couldn't recall what it could be or exactly when the behaviour started. We tried varying degrees of wideness and speed in our door

openings, and the trigger seemed to be as soon as the hand went onto the freezer handle. Her Maltese, in true lapdog fashion and not to be left on his own, followed his mistress around the house like a little shadow, often tripping her up, save when she reached for the freezer. In order to stop the fleeing, I put the dog on a lead and approached the fridge/freezer. Before I opened the freezer door I gave him a treat, then I put my hand on the door handle and gave another treat. We repeated this a few times. I wanted him completely comfortable before even attempting to open the door. He was a little hesitant at first, but sausage bits soon won him round. I then opened the freezer door very slowly, just a crack, and gave him another treat. We repeated this over and over. I wanted the freezer door to represent something positive instead of negative. The owner was to repeat this on a daily basis until the dog stopped trying to flee.

As I was leaving, my client's cleaner walked into the kitchen. We were briefly introduced. She was Italian and didn't speak much English. Neither did my client speak much Italian. I had studied in Padova for a year, where the girl was from, so we had a quick exchange (in Italian) about the city. I explained why I was in the house, and she let out a little "Ah!" She told me that some months ago, when she had gone to put the ice trays back in the freezer, a tub of ice cream had fallen out and landed on the dog at her feet. She hadn't thought much more of it. I relayed this to my client, who let out another slow "Ahhh!" Mystery solved.

Case Study 2
A friend with a Labradoodle reported some strange behaviour in her dog, who had recently become very skittish and jumpy.

Common Problems and How to Fix Them

He was an extreme fidget, and no longer tolerated hands coming towards his face – he'd started to snap at them. He would suddenly turn his head 90 degrees and then turn it the other way, even when there were no hands approaching. He would hide without apparent cause or reason. He seemed to be scared by loud noises and would go into a 'freeze' stance, refusing to move. Other times he would whizz around and occasionally bump into objects.

I paid them an informal visit. I already knew the dog, and the dog knew me. After our usual friendly greeting I did a few exercises with him, command and response type, to build a bit of a bond. I normally wait until I have eye contact before offering any kind of reward, but I found it hard to see if he was looking at me or not. His hair had grown quite a bit since I last saw him, and it now flopped over his eyes. If I couldn't see him properly, presumably he couldn't see me. Then it dawned on me that this was probably the root cause of all his strange behaviours.

I had had a session with a blind dog once. His brain had failed to develop visual acuity, so he relied much more on sound and became very sensitive to it. He would react to sounds no one else could hear and overreact to some sounds we could hear, which made him rather erratic in his behaviour. My friend's dog was beginning to show some similar signs. I suggested the first thing we try was a haircut. She was then to work on getting eye contact frequently, and the minute she couldn't see his eyes, get out the nail scissors. Remarkably, my friend reported only a few days later that her dog was back to his normal self.

Any of the 'poo'/ 'oodle' mixes, or dogs with bushy eyebrows, can be affected, so keep a lookout. Even a long beard can impinge a dog's movement. Getting in and out of cars or any kind of agility could prove difficult if he is always treading on his beard. This could be perceived as stubbornness if you are not wised-up.

Case Study 3

I had a telephone consultation with the owner of a Lhasa apso. The owner lived too far away for me to make a home visit, and because I had been recommended, I didn't want to decline the job. In brief, the dog barked and howled every time the owners opened a bottle of wine. Quite amusing really. I could do with one of those to keep me on the straight and narrow. Lhasa apsos were bred to guard monasteries in Tibet. They have very acute hearing. I imagine that the noise of the corkscrew turning, and the subsequent popping of the cork set him off. I asked how the owners reacted when this happened. Of course, it was their party trick, especially when they had guests round and all found it highly amusing. That was the problem, right there. The laughter in itself would be perceived by the dog as encouragement and approval. Instead, I told them to get eye contact with the dog as the corkscrew was going in, and correct with a "tshh" the moment they thought the dog was going to bark: catch it early, before a noise had even been uttered. They would be correcting the dog's thought process. But more importantly, they had to mean it, otherwise it wouldn't work. This was not a serious behavioural issue, and I think they were simply curious as to why it happened. I'm not sure they were actually keen to reverse the behaviour or to lose their dinner party entertainment.

Case Study 4

I don't know why it is, but recently I have seen quite a few older couples with young border collies and I can't help wondering if the owners have the energy to provide the exercise and stimulation this breed so badly needs. A couple I met in Oxfordshire whilst on a walk were no exception. We often walked the same route and had passed each other many times and exchanged pleasantries. My dogs would be running around off lead, whilst theirs was always on a short lead, in the middle of the countryside. I felt rather sorry for it.

During one encounter, the conversation as usual turned to our dogs. I was berating the poor recall of my dog when any wildlife was around. They said that was nothing in comparison to their mad dog who would jump up and bite the walls in their house. I took that as my cue to tell them my profession. They didn't seem to think they had a problem, until I explained their dog's strange behaviour could be the result of understimulation. I agreed to go round that evening to see if there was anything I could do.

I was ushered into the living room and presented with a cup of tea. The husband sat in his chair by the window and Lupin, as the dog was called, lay down at our feet. They joked that her nickname was loopy Lupin, but I instinctively felt they were underestimating and undermining her. The wife was a very chatty Welsh lady and launched into a full life history beginning with their first dog some 30 years ago. It seemed I might be here some time.

Mid-way into her monologue, Lupin suddenly sprang up and launched herself at the wall in front of us. It was the most extraordinary thing to witness. Then she spun around a few times, and ended up just staring at the wall.

"There you go, Fenella. Mad as a hatter. Didn't I tell you? Now you know what we're on about."

I knew collies were very adept at gaining their owner's attention, but could this really be such an elaborate ruse? And if it were, how on earth did it originate? While these thoughts were running through my head, the sun came out from behind a cloud, and for a second a small light reflection danced on the wall opposite. I looked around to see where the light might be bouncing off. As the husband took another sip of his tea, it happened again. "Do that again", I chirped.

"Do what?"

"Raise your hand to your face."

Nothing.

"Now wiggle it around."

Sure enough, there was a little spark of light projected onto the wall. We deduced that the husband's watch had been refracting the sunlight, streaming in from the window, onto the wall opposite, directly in front of where Lupin lay. Her natural desire to play and chase would have made her leap at it; even try and herd it. In the absence of any light reflections, if she was bored, she could easily mimic the same behaviour, as it always seemed to provoke them into giving her attention.

Quite a list of circumstances had to line up for me to fathom this one out – the husband had to be wearing his watch, he had to be sitting in his chair by the window, he had to take a sip of his tea just as the sun came out, and Lupin had to be in the room – so thank you, powers that be.

I explained to the couple that Lupin was not loopy. She was highly intelligent. But she was bored. She needed daily mental games to keep her occupied, and a natural outlet for her herding tendencies. I recommended some agility classes and some time off lead to drain some physical energy too. I have been helping them teach Lupin to come back to the whistle, as they were anxious about losing her on walks. They also had to stop the wall jumping as it was an unhealthy fixation. They were not to react when she did it, and redirect her onto a different game or toy, giving her positive feedback. They report she is doing well. I just hope they have the energy to keep up the good work.

PART THREE

Keeping on the Right Path

Now you have all the knowledge to 'fix' your dog, and you have put it into place, it would be a shame to let it slide. As long as you stick to your new behaviour, the dog will stick to his.

Every now and again, I get a phone call or an email a few months after seeing a client, and they explain that after my visit everything changed for the better and the dog was very responsive to the new protocol. However, now the dog has back-tracked a little, and he's not responding the way he did after I left. My first question is, "Have *you* back-tracked in *your* behaviour?" And the answer is always the same.

Dogs need the consistency of any new rules or behaviour for them to be successful, and that means 100% of the time. If you are in a hurry one day, or too tired another day, or lose your temper, or skip the walk, it will all have a knock-on effect. Basically, it's never the dog!

Keep up the good work, be consistent and consider these following topics to get the most out of your newly behaved friend, for the long term.

CHAPTER 20
To Neuter or Not to Neuter

This is a heated topic which almost everyone has an opinion on. And each will come at it from their own angle. Vets will see the physical pros and cons; which diseases are more prevalent after neutering and which are diminished. Dog rescue workers will no doubt only see the benefits of neutering, as it will stop the increase of more unwanted pets. A behaviourist will be concerned about how neutering will affect a dog's state of mind and his subsequent actions. The owner may simply just do what the vet recommends, or listen to hearsay, perhaps without all the facts. I have overheard many a conversation along the lines of, "Well, we're having him done because he's getting aggressive", or "Well, it's what responsible owners do isn't it?"

The fact is, there is no 'one size fits all' answer. It may depend on the temperament of the dog or their age or whether they live with another dog, and what that relationship is like and whether that dog is neutered. Sometimes it can depend on the breed. For example, spaniel rage is significantly higher in neutered spaniels. We need to take into account any strange behaviours a dog might be exhibiting, such as mounting or licking another dog's genitals repeatedly.

I will set out what I have gleaned from various studies, seminars and research, and give you an abridged version of the results, without going into too much detail. First, I'll cover the physical pros and cons, and then the behavioural ones.

Neutering Pros (physical)

- For a female, probably the most obvious plus for an owner would be no more coming into season. Around twice a year (3 times for smaller dogs), an entire female will come 'on heat'. Generally speaking, she bleeds for around 2 weeks and during this time she can become pregnant if mating occurs. Anyone who has lived with a bitch in oestrus will know how inconvenient it is having to confine your dog to the kitchen, where floors can be mopped easily, and keeping her on lead when out and sticking to remote walks where she is less likely to attract the attention of wandering males. Those of you who have followed my advice and not allowed their dog on the furniture will be thankful in this instance.
- No unwanted litters of puppies.
- No health risks associated with giving birth, such as dystocia (obstructed birth).
- Male dogs naturally have an urge to mate around every 6 weeks. This can lead to frustration and restlessness if these needs aren't met, so neutering can be considered kinder to pent-up males.

- Prevention of cancers and diseases of the mammary glands, ovaries and womb (such as pyometra, a fatal womb infection) in females, and of the testicles and prostate in males. (If a male has undescended testes, he should be neutered to prevent them becoming cancerous, which would otherwise almost always become inevitable.)
- Research suggests spayed females live longer. However, this may be due to owners who spay their dogs, caring for them in ways other owners don't.

Neutering Cons (physical)

- Risk from the surgery itself.
- Increased appetite and therefore risk of obesity and need for weight management.
- If a female is neutered before her first season, it can increase incontinence in later life, cystitis and joint problems. My 14-year-old Lab was spayed aged 6 months as part of the adoption process. She developed early-onset arthritis, and is now severely riddled with it in her hips, knees and elbows. She also wets her bed when asleep.
- If either gender is neutered too early (under 6 months), the growth plates in their joints don't close properly and they can become quite leggy. This can lead to musculoskeletal problems such as orthopaedic disease.

- Higher risk of lymphoma, skin tumours and other diseases.
- Higher risk of hip dysplasia, noise phobias and anxiety.
- Neutered males may give off confusing chemical signals and become victims of other males' mounting behaviour. If the neutered male learns that the only way to protect himself is by growling and biting, because his owner is not stepping in, then this can become ingrained behaviour.

Neutering Pros (behavioural)

- Can help a dog take less risks and be less competitive with other dogs. It's important to note that taking risks (eg. putting paws on another dog's shoulders, bullying, rushing up to another dog in greeting) and succeeding in those risks, is an addictive habit, and it increases the production of testosterone, not the other way round. It's not the production of testosterone which causes a dog to take risks.
- May help mounting and excessive or inappropriate scent marking.
- May help conflict between two males or two females living together.
- May improve recall when involved in play with other dogs.
- No risk of phantom pregnancy behaviours in females.

Neutering Cons (behavioural)

- May become aggressive or make an aggressive dog *worse.*
- May make a fearful or anxious male dog more fearful .
- Loss of confidence.
- It may not affect a behaviour if that behaviour has become ingrained and the dog has learnt that it makes them feel good (eg. mounting or aggression).
- Unneutered male dogs show a slower cognitive decline with age. In short, keep your balls, keep your marbles!

Let us remember that each case must be put into context, and decisions must be made on an individual basis. What might benefit one dog, may have detrimental results in another. Do get advice from your vet and behaviourist before automatically giving your dog the snip.

Case study 1

I was called to Northamptonshire, to the home of a lovely couple in their sixties and their handsome, male, black Labrador, Nero. They lived in a large house with extensive gardens, surrounded by fields and countryside. Nero was unmistakeably male, with a wide face, stocky frame and muscular legs. At 2 years of age, he was at peak fitness. The lady owner started with a familiar patter – "He's the perfect dog and really very sweet, but…" She went on to describe how every time they met another dog when out on a walk,

Nero would go charging up to them, whether they were willing participants or not, and regardless of their sex, he would try and mount them. While this was a source of great embarrassment to her, I got the feeling she was slightly proud of owning a testosterone-fuelled stud. She had no plans to breed from him, but felt that a man should be a man, and be able to keep his balls. I asked what she had tried so far to curb the behaviour.

"Well, I just march on and pretend not to see!" She also admitted to pretending to be a little deaf as well, so she could ignore the calls of the other owners to come and get her dog off.

In the absence of any intervention, and by ignoring the behaviour, she was allowing it. Nero was getting a high from his risky behaviour, which triggered the production of more testosterone. Because they lived on a huge plot of private land, the dog was mostly walked within the confines of this space, and therefore hardly ever met other dogs and dog walkers.

No wonder he would then seek to repeat his high on the rare occasion he saw another dog. He saw a valuable resource, and went to claim it. And because this resource was rare, it made it even more important to have while he had the chance.

We went for a walk so I could observe Nero and his owner's behaviour. I also wanted to drain some of his energy before introducing him to Willa. (Willa is my 14-year-old very placid, non-reactive, neutered Labrador. She is a very good judge of character where other dogs are concerned, and I use her reaction to gauge how stable or unstable another dog is.) I suggested we walk on a public footpath. Nero was never on a lead, as his owner saw no need for one. I put him on a long lead so he would be free to act as normal, but I could rein him in if I needed to. Sure enough, on the first sighting of another dog, Nero rushed over, tail high and quivering in excitement, head high and ears pricked. With very little sniffing, which would have been the polite way to say hello, he tried to mount the other dog, who as it turned out was a neutered male, who told Nero in no uncertain terms to lay off. Nero was undeterred, but I called a halt to the meeting at this point. There was no apology from my client to the owner of the other dog, just laughter. Well, I saw the main part of the problem right there. Even if this was embarrassed, nervous laughter, it was encouraging Nero to carry on doing what he was doing, as it obviously made his owner happy.

On our return to the house, I got Willa out of the car and let her have a sniff around.

If Nero acted inappropriately around an old lady, he was clearly reading the signals wrongly. He was very overexcited to see her, but I introduced him from a distance, so he would have to use his nose. I did not allow him closer until he had calmed down a bit. His hormones had taken over his brain and he wasn't going to listen to any vocal commands, so I had to use a lot of touch corrections. Even as I stood between Nero and Willa, he was still intent on pestering her. Willa growled at him a few times to show her displeasure. I spared Willa the unwanted attention and took Nero away. He had to learn that no introductions would take place if he went in full throttle.

It was clear to me that Nero was a sex pest, driven by his hormones, and at an age when testosterone production is at its peak. Having him neutered would almost definitely help. Once neutered, I suggested longer walks to drain some of that exuberance, and walks with other dogs so he could be properly socialised and feel he was part of a pack. I also advised his owner to keep him on a long line at first, to control meetings, and told her to disagree with any unwanted advances, not ignore them.

Although reticent at first, she finally succumbed to having him neutered after a particularly nasty encounter where both dogs ended up in fisticuffs. Nero is now a happy dog, free from the frustrations of wanting to mate continually.

There are many reasons why a dog may mount or hump another dog, or human. It does not automatically mean they should be marched down the vet to be neutered, but if the behaviour is perceived to come from being over sexed and frustrated, then neutering may be the best thing to do for your dog, and so sparing their 'victim'.

Mounting behaviour and why dogs do it:

- It feels good.
- Because it feels good, it's reinforced. Nature's way of insuring reproduction.
- In play.
- It's a motor pattern that needs to be practised.
- Scent exchange. Dogs in the same pack want to smell the same.
- Arousal.
- Used as a low level threat – may lead to conflict if it's non-consensual. Risk-taking behaviour that some old-school behaviourists label as dominance.

- Used as a strategy to get attention or to get something to happen.
- A symptom of confusing chemical signals, usually given off by the neutered male mountee (ie. the neutered male smells more like a female, which can arouse the unneutered male).

Case study 2

Archie was a male, English bull terrier cross. He was huge and very strong. He was an unneutered 18-month-old when I first met him. He had been rescued from a military base in Eastern Europe, where he was kept in an enclosure on a long chain all day, to deter any intruders. He was not walked or socialised intentionally, to keep him mean. Archie's owner over previous years had also rescued several other large breeds, including a male Great Dane, a male Rottweiler and a female Doberman, who were still part of the household.

The problem presented to me was that Archie was aggressive to the other dogs in his household, aggressive to other dogs on walks and aggressive to humans. He was impossible to walk because of his constant reactivity, and he pulled so hard on the lead he would pull his owner over and choke himself. He had to be kept segregated from the rest of the pack at all times, otherwise a fight would break out.

"Do I really want to take this case on?", I thought.

I was curious. On my first meeting with the family, Archie was barking away behind the kitchen door as I stepped into the hallway, and I was met by the other three enormous dogs who came charging at me full throttle, jumping up and not so much sniffing, as poking me. Not aggressive, but very rude behaviour and rather intimidating. There was clearly a lack of rules in the home. I was told that to avoid confrontations Archie was walked at 5am. He was too strong for the wife, so if the husband was unwell (he had been having some health issues), he didn't get walked at all. No outlet for all that pent-up energy.

After a short chat, I asked the husband to meet me outside their house with Archie on a muzzle. The owner's wife had, after all, told me with some certainty, "He *will* bite you".

We walked in parallel some four metres apart, and I gradually got closer. I allowed him to sniff me without paying him any attention. After a few minutes I glanced down at him and met his gaze. That was too much for him and he barked nervously, and immediately retreated. I didn't back away – I didn't want to empower him. What I saw was a very unsure dog, who had turned to aggression as his only recourse for keeping perceived threats away. He couldn't run away to avoid the threat as he was always on a short lead.

Pretty quickly, I was able to get him walking on a slack lead. He responded well to the new relaxed energy the other end of the lead, and to a vocal 'uhuh' correction when he pulled ahead. We did share more eye contact and treats, and I even trusted him enough mid-way through the session to remove the muzzle, which put him in a more natural state of mind. He was reactive to other dogs, so I showed the owner some distraction techniques which worked well. I wanted to not even give him the chance to react, as the lunging and barking was fuelling more testosterone, and also fuelling a vicious cycle of more lunging and barking. The longer period of time he could go without reacting, the more new positive neural pathways would be formed, so at this point, avoidance through distraction was the first step.

The owner's desired outcome was to reunite Archie with the rest of the pack, but this was a way down the line yet. He was keen to get Archie neutered, but I wasn't sure if this was the right course of action, as it can often actually increase aggression. It almost certainly would have made him more fearful. What this dog needed was some confidence-building, at least one other walk a day (ideally off lead in an enclosed area with no other dogs around), and some clear direction from his owner, who by the way was just the man for the job and very measured and calm. But he was fairly adamant about the neutering, so what I ended up suggesting was reversable chemical castration. Suprelorin is an injected implant which renders the dog infertile for around 6 months, and the dog behaves as a castrated dog would. This way, we could revert Archie to his original fertile state if he reacted badly or if it made no difference at all.

Archie is a sweet dog who I am very fond of, and have seen a few times since. The Suprelorin did not have a marked difference on his behaviour, but the owner did report mild increased anxiety and aggression, so has decided to let things be. I didn't see them for seven months after our first session, so it's hard to tell whether the dip in behaviour was all down to the Suprelorin, or a lapse in the behaviour training, as the owner did get sick again.

But with increased frequency of sessions, we are making progress, and Archie has even sniffed a few other dogs hello without reacting, and has walked out successfully with Willa and the female Doberman of his household.

Archie learning to walk without pulling. We adopted the figure of eight lead configuration around his nose at first, for his owner to have extra control.

CHAPTER 21
Diet

This is another area of huge debate and controversy. I am not a nutritionist, but I will tell you what I believe to be the best diet for your dog, based on what has worked for me, and backed up by (some but not all) professionals.

Dogs are carnivores. You can tell by their teeth. Long pointy canines for tearing and chewing meat. None of their teeth are flat topped, like a cow's for example, who uses its teeth and jaw in a sideways motion to break down the cellulose in plants to make it digestible. Some would argue that dogs are omnivores. While they *can* indeed eat 'everything' (save a few things which are poisonous to them like chocolate, onions, artificial sweetener, alcohol), much of what they *can* eat is indigestible. They don't have the teeth or the jaw action to chew and grind food and break it down. Dogs tend to swallow their food in a gulp. Carbohydrates put pressure on a dog's pancreas as it struggles to digest the indigestible.

Grains and soya are also hard for a dog to digest, and can cause allergies, as the immune system is severely compromised. They don't need any carbs – so that's vegetables, fruits and grains. You would do well to check the ingredients and their quantities on your pack of dog food to see just how much of it is actually protein and how much is being padded out with cheap unnecessary carbs. A little fruit and veg won't do your dog any harm, but they will only do your dog some good if they are blitzed, ground or pulsed, to break down the cellulose, so the nutrients can be absorbed. Rule is, if you can see the bits of veg when they go in, you'll be seeing them again when they come out the other end.

I would like to see over half the content be protein. One of my clients was a vegetarian, and made her dog eat vegetarian too. This may have been in her best interests, but it certainly wasn't in the dog's. She was compromising the dog's health. When we take a dog into our home, we owe it to them to give them what they need, not what we need, in the form of diet, exercise, and enrichment.

The bottom line is, dogs need meat. This is what they would choose in the wild. And they would consume the raw meat along with bones, cartilage and hair. All plays a part in keeping the dog healthy, and their immune systems up to scratch. Dogs' teeth have not evolved since becoming domesticated, so why should we presume that their stomachs have?

Whether you feed raw, dry kibble, canned meat or fry up the best sirloin steak, your dog needs variety. He should be eating 6-7 species ie. chicken, beef, duck, salmon, venison, pork, turkey, lamb. Not only will it stop him getting bored of his food, but also it's better for maintaining a healthy gut and digestive system. Fussy eaters may just be bored of eating the same old thing day in day out. Besides varying the flavours, you could 'animate' the food to make it more appealing. By

Keeping on the Right Path

this I mean pick a bit of it up in your hands (yes, even if it is raw tripe) and throw it across the garden or kitchen floor. Your dog can practise catching it in his mouth, or chasing it across the floor. It is also a form of early recall, as your dog will naturally gravitate back to you for more. Use mealtimes to bond with your dog. Ask for eye contact before every mouthful, or put a handful on the ground and ask him to stay until you give your release command. I have seen dogs who only eat home cooked food, suddenly come alive and eat an entire meal of kibble when the food was animated and the owner became involved with mealtimes in a fun and appealing way. So think about *how* you are feeding, as well as *what* you are feeding.

You will notice that dogs fed on dried kibble have large, smelly poo. All the grain and veg they can't digest is shovelled along their digestive system and out the other end. Ever fed your dog sweetcorn? It comes out whole. Zero nutrition, maximum waste. Some cheap kibbles are highly processed, contain additives, and have very little protein in them. Even the ones boasting 50% protein (usually labelled as meat derivatives) or more can be dubious, as protein can be the toenail clippings from a cow. Even shoe leather is protein. Look on the label and trust the brands that tell you exactly what the protein is. Keep away from foods with E numbers and artificial preservatives. Often, I have found that the worst dog foods have the cutest pictures of dogs on the packaging, and the best have no pictures at all.

The same rule applies to dog treats. Look at the label, and try and feed snacks that are 100% meat. Stay clear of rawhide. Rawhide is dried animal skin. It may seem natural enough, but the skins are then soaked in highly concentrated salt baths, lime and chemicals to prolong their life. Rawhide is not easily digestible and if your dog swallows chunks of it, it can sit in his stomach for months causing gastrointestinal problems. There is also a risk of obstruction if your dog does not fully chew and break down the rawhide before swallowing.

Cooked bones are also dangerous. They can easily splinter and puncture the oesophageal lining. Give raw bones as an occasional treat, and supervise the eating, especially if around another dog. Raw bones are highly prized and can cause a fight.

I recently had a puppy to stay, who came with his food for the day. The packaging was tasteful and appealing (and yes there was a cute puppy on the front – warning sign!), and the contents were expensive. The label boasted 'high protein content'. Not high in my opinion. There was 38% turkey, only 4% of which was freshly prepared; the rest, dried powder, which consisted of goodness knows what. It also boasted 'hypoallergenic'. The only thing I could find that was hypoallergenic about it was that it didn't contain wheat, soya or gluten. However, in its place was 43% rice and oats: bad carbohydrates for dogs, especially in these quantities. And then of course the remaining 19% was packed out with cheap veg – more indigestible carbohydrates. I'm being harsh – it did have omega 3 supplement, which is healthy. All 0.04% of it. Suffice to say, I have never seen such a large poo come out of such a small body. So high was the 'waste' content of his food. Shameful really, since puppies, more than adult dogs, need a particularly high protein content in their diet, as they are still growing and their organs are still developing.

Problems that can relate to a poor diet include:

- Eating their own or another dog's excrement
- Hyperactivity
- Eating toilet paper, soil, roots, twigs
- Excessive scratching
- Unhealthy coat – dull and dandruff
- Hair loss
- Runny stools

I feed my dogs raw meat. That's 80% meat, 10% offal, 10% bone and cartilage. Even some vets throw their hands in the air at this. All that live salmonella! The fact is, a dog fed raw meat (and fish) will automatically adjust his stomach enzymes to it. These enzymes are 'bionic' compared to the enzymes of a kibble-fed dog. They destroy any harmful bacteria. This puts your dog at an advantage when they lick something a few days old, smushed into the pavement. When meat is cooked, the bacteria which help to build up the strength of the stomach acid are killed. So raw really is best. A raw diet is also available in freeze dried form, which resembles kibble, and can be useful for travelling or if you don't have enough freezer space for fresh meat.

If you do decide to switch to raw, which I highly recommend, go to a raw dog food supplier, not your butcher, so you know your dog is getting the right balance of meat and bone. Meat without bits of raw bone may give your dog loose stools. Too much bone may make him constipated. Never mix raw with kibble. They are digested differently. Kibble takes longer to go through the dog's system, so would slow down the digestion of the raw food, and allow bacteria to flourish.

Other advantages of feeding raw are smaller, harder, less smelly stools, less smelly breath, less flatulence, less allergies, cleaner teeth, healthy immune system, shiny coat, less water needed. When I switched my Labrador to raw, she lost her abnormal yeasty odour and stopped scratching within a matter of days. I have never looked back.

Dogs who are eating strange things such as toilet paper, are desperately trying to give their bodies the nutrients they crave. Their diet is deficient. Many dog foods are packaged and coloured to appeal to the human. Left to the dog, he would probably steer well clear.

Case Study

A young lady called me for help with her exuberant chocolate Labrador. She reported that he had recently become extra hyper and greedy beyond compare, and would eat food off the table if her back was turned, or pounce on any morsel if it fell on the floor. He would snatch food out of her children's hands, and was a scavenge when on walks, going from bin to bin, bench to bench. He was aptly named Dyson.

We met at the house first so I could assess the situation. Dyson bounded to the door and excitedly barked and jumped all over me, even though I paid him no attention. His owner met me with a toddler on her hip, and another crying at her feet, and was flustered and apologetic. I had purposefully come at lunch time to see Dyson at his worst, and as if on cue he jumped up to snatch a soggy biscuit out of the younger child's hand. The child shrieked, mum yelled at the dog, who then knocked the standing child over. This was all in the first thirty seconds of being there. Oh, and did I mention there was another dog in the house, just to add to the chaos?

I asked to observe a normal walk to the park. This poor lady had her hands full, juggling between getting two children suited and booted, one in a buggy and one in a sling, and the dogs on leads. It was no wonder there was very little energy left to give Dyson the attention he needed to make a calm exit. He pulled them across the road and down the street to the park. Once off lead he made a beeline for the bin and stuck his head right in. Then he caught sight of a man eating a sandwich leaving the park, and followed him out of the gates. Mum was yelling his name over and over, arms flailing, running towards him, with a buggy and toddler in tow. She gasped at me, "You see – this is what I'm up against". I really felt for her. Dyson was not a tricky case in my eyes, and certainly not a bad dog, but it would be tricky for her to give him the one-to-one he needed. I calmly called him and walked away from him, as I fed the other dog a tasty treat. This had the desired effect of getting Dyson to bound over, fearful of missing out.

I noticed Dyson's coat was rather dull and flaky, and that he had thinning patches of hair on his hind legs. He was rather plump and apparently always hungry. I asked about diet. He was on a cheap brand of kibble with little protein and high grain content. The other dog didn't seem to be suffering on it. Was there anything Dyson was on that the other wasn't, I asked. As it turned out, he was on a course of steroids for his skin condition. I immediately looked up the side effects of the steroids and one of them was increased appetite. Poor Dyson was going round in circles – he was being given a poor diet, which no doubt was giving him the skin condition in the first place, then he was being given medication for the skin condition which increased his hunger, and made him eat more of the poorly nourished food, contributing to his bad skin. It wasn't Dyson's fault that he had become hungry, or that he had become hyper. His food was full of additives that would have had him running around in circles – a bit like a small child after a bag of sweets. Quite frankly I was surprised he wasn't eating his own poo as well! This is what some dogs do in a desperate bid to get the minerals and vitamins they need.

I suggested they put Dyson on a raw diet for a month and stop the steroids, with the OK from the vet. I also suggested he be taken out more frequently, to lessen the 'cabin fever' feeling and drain some of that boisterous energy. I showed her how to stop Dyson going for food which was dropped on the floor, by teaching him some impulse control. And he could do it. Easily. The hard bit for her was going to be following through with the training, given all the other distractions she had to contend with.

I saw them six weeks later. Dyson was still the same friendly, enthusiastic dog, but he looked different. The hair had grown back and his coat was clear. His owner had reported that she still had problems containing his excitement at the door (she hadn't had time to practice what I'd taught her), but he was less manic in and out of the house, and less of a scavenge. Well, I call that a result.

A note on food in general is to always, wherever possible, feed your dog after exercise. Reasons being:

- It will give him a reason to come back to you, and back home. Especially useful for dogs with poor recall.

Keeping on the Right Path

- It will incentivise him to eat, as he will have worked for it.
- He will be hungrier as he will have worked up an appetite. If he is hungry, he will eat a full meal, and so have a full belly, and so be in a resting state for a couple of hours afterwards, allowing you to go out or get on with work.
- Food is better digested when you are in a resting state. Hence the phrase 'rest and digest'. You wouldn't go out on a run after a Sunday roast, would you? Poorly digested food can lead to vomiting, bloating, gas and constipation or diarrhoea.

Never leave food down. As I explained in greater detail in chapter 3 on rules, it leads to demotivation and erratic blood sugar levels. Also, if your dog does not eat a full meal in one go, he will not be in a resting state afterwards. Not good for skittish or hyperactive dogs.

If you have a dog who bolts his food as if he hasn't eaten in weeks, you could try hand feeding some or all of it. Or throw it across the kitchen floor or garden for him to sniff out. Eating a bit slower will aid digestion and prevent any discomfort afterwards. If you have multiple dogs, feed them in separate rooms, so they can take their time, without the primal fear that another dog is going to steal their prize. Another option would be to reintroduce 3 meals a day. This will help regulate the blood sugar and keep hunger spikes at bay. For the same reason I would avoid feeding only once a day.

CHAPTER 22
Mental Stimulation

All dogs, no matter what breed or age, need *mental* as well as physical exercise. Not only does it drain energy, so keeping them calm and balanced, but it enriches their lives by giving them something meaningful to do. Young dogs in particular need mental activities to drain some of that youthful exuberance. Old, infirm or injured dogs, or dogs recovering from surgery need more mental stimulation as their physical exercise will be considerably reduced. Certain 'intelligent' breeds and working dogs need a mountain of mental stimulation to keep them satisfied. You should be carving out huge chunks of your day devising new challenges for them. Too often have I seen a working cocker in a family environment, living in a flat in the city, with a myriad of problems that could have been solved by a) giving the dog a job, and b) choosing the correct breed for your lifestyle in the first place.

Mental challenges alleviate boredom and frustration and will stop destructiveness when you are out. Leave your dog a food ball or puzzle when you leave, so he has something to do other than sit on his bed or bark at the squirrels outside the window. This simple act can also stave off depression and keep your dog happier. A daily brain workout will stop the onset of cognitive disfunction, just as in humans. Stress levels reduce when a dog is mentally stimulated, which have a knock-on effect of also lowering levels of aggression. If you have an aggressive dog, give that energy a different outlet and involve him in using his nose to hunt out treats. A mental workout before bedtime will have your dog sleeping better and not waking up at the crack of dawn. And if all that wasn't reason enough, playing games with your dog will vastly increase the loving bond you have and bring trust and fulfilment. The stronger the bond, the more obedient he will be.

If you find yourself unable to take your dog out for a walk one day, make sure he gets a couple of good sessions of brainwork. A 10 minute play session will drain as much energy as a 20 minute walk. Dogs get bored of everything staying the same, so even a change of scenery can be stimulating. Surprise him occasionally with a new place to play, or with a new toy or game.

There are plenty of books out there and YouTube videos dedicated to brain games for dogs, so use these resources. Ideally you should try and engage your dog's grey matter on a daily basis. Interactive games are best for independent dogs. Ideally you don't want him to have too much fun without you – like the dog who rushes off to amuse himself as soon as you get to the park. For the dog who follows you round the house from room to room, and may have separation issues, build confidence with non-interactive games. Chuck some treats on a snuffle mat and then walk away. He will enjoy these short moments of independence. Feeling good on his own.

Below are a few ideas of both interactive and non-interactive games to get you going. Start easy and progress to harder. Never let your dog fail. If he starts scratching or yawning, walks off or looks around him, instead of focusing on the task, then he is confused and doesn't know what he is supposed to do, so take a step back and make it easier. Always end the session with him succeeding. We want him to feel good about himself.

If it's a new trick you are teaching, it's useful to have a clicker to mark the desired behaviour with a click and then reward. If not, then mark the desired behaviour with a 'yes', and then reward. The advantage of a clicker is that it is a neutral sound which belies any over excitement or frustration.

- Teach a new trick. Sit, lie down, stay, paw, touch, roll over, spin, play dead, leg weave, beg, bark, fetch, tidy away your toys, shut the door, open the door, bring me the remote control – the list is endless. Do what comes naturally to your dog and you will have a better success rate. I challenged myself with my fearful rescue, and had him playing a guitar he was scared of, and retrieving objects although he didn't have a retrieving bone in his body. If you can turn something he views as negative into something positive (ie. if the reward is good enough), you are increasing his confidence. This is called counter conditioning.
- Use what nature has given us as an obstacle course. Get your dog to jump on tree stumps and over branches. Throw his ball into bushes for him to find. Or get him to jump over a park bench and then under it. Or set up an obstacle course in your garden.

Keeping on the Right Path

- Play hide and seek. Hide behind a tree or in tall grass and call his name, or hide under a pile of cushions in another room and call his name. Finding you will be reward enough.
- Play catch me – run round a bush or tree stump and see if he can figure out that it may be easier to catch you if he turns and goes in the opposite direction.
- Anything that has him using his nose is draining energy. Throw treats into long grass for him to sniff out.
- Hide treats around the room as he sits and watches you, then tell him to go find them.
- Lay a scent trail for him. I tie a sausage on a piece of string and drag it along the ground to its hiding place, then move away and get him to follow the trail.
- Vary the feeding methods of his meals: in a food ball, thrown across the kitchen floor, in a snuffle mat, by hand and giving you eye contact between each mouthful.
- Cover a treat or food bowl with a tea towel and see if he can figure out how to remove the tea towel to get to the food. Progress to using a towel, then a sheet, then an upturned cardboard box.
- Put treats in a cardboard egg box with the lid closed. Let him rip it up to get inside.
- Fill a bucket or cardboard box with empty drink cans or plastic bottles and scrunched up newspaper and toss in some treats. The cans will be a good challenge for a fearful dog, as they will be noisy.

- Put treats under tennis balls in a muffin tray.
- Put treats under upturned plastic cups.
- Teach your dog the names of his toys.
- Practise impulse control exercises. Ask your dog to stay as you throw a treat or toy down. Then tell him "Get it".

Use your imagination. Nothing I have suggested costs any money, so no need to go out and buy expensive dog puzzles. If you have totally run out of ideas, simply play with your dog in whatever way comes naturally to you, and in whichever way he responds positively to. He should want to engage with you. Keep play sessions short. You don't want to overstimulate him. Leave a box of toys out for your dog to choose which one he would like to play with, but rotate the toys, keeping at least half of them away in a cupboard, so he never gets bored of them.

Mahler sniffing out a piece of cheese under two of the tennis balls.

Keeping on the Right Path

Teaching Rocky to play the guitar.

Teaching my 3 month old spaniel cross puppy to shut the door.

CHAPTER 23
The Walk

The single most important thing you can do for your dog is to walk him. It is part of the solution to almost every single problem listed. It should be a pleasurable experience for owner and dog. And no, having a big back garden doesn't cut the mustard. Thinking your dog won't need a walk because he's been wandering around all day in the garden is misguided. Your dog needs new sights, new smells, new people, new dogs to stimulate him. Moreover, dogs are migratory animals. They are tuned to following a leader; a leader who will lead them across plains to water, food and shelter. When a dog is in following/travelling mode, he is relaxed and trusting. His ears are back and his tail is mid-way (not high or low). This is what we want to see when out walking our dogs. He should be at your side, mirroring your every move. If you stop, he will stop; if you move forward, he will move forward. No words are necessary. It is pure harmonious movement. For me, the image springs to mind of a waltzing couple, with one of the pair leading every step and the other following in sync.

The walk is not a passive affair. Nor should it, in an ideal world, be utilised as a multitasking outing. In reality, of course we take the dog on the school run, or to the shops, but what I am saying is, don't disconnect from your dog on those outings. I often see people walking their dog, chatting on their mobile, or playing with their kids in the playground. The dog is forgotten and is doing his own thing. We're all guilty of this at times. Just be aware and reconnect.

As I said in chapter 7 on lead pulling, do not underestimate the power of the walk on a lead. You are physically and mentally connected, and it's a perfect time to give direction and bond with your dog.

Whatever your dog's breed, I recommend taking him for a walk twice a day. One longer one (45 mins to an hour) and one shorter one (20 mins to half an hour). I would call this the minimum requirement. Some breeds will need much more. If your dog is young, he will need more. If your dog is high energy, he will need more. If you cannot commit to this every day for the next 10 or so years, then you should rethink embarking on this journey.

Of course, there are exceptions: if your dog is constantly triggered by his outside environment, or if he is old or in poor health. Then you need to manage the walks accordingly. Play more sniffing games inside to drain energy. Young puppies too need less walking. The formula for puppy walking is: multiply his age in months by 5, and then give him this amount of walking twice a day (ie, a 4-month-old puppy will need 4 x 5 = 20 minutes exercise, twice a day). Over-walking small puppies can damage their developing joints. Much bonding and mental stimulation can be done within the home and garden. This does not mean you can't take your puppy outside to just watch the world go by. He will be learning from sniffing, listening and looking at new stimuli.

If your puppy has not had all its vaccinations, it is advised not to put him on the ground, which can harbour some nasty viruses. Take him out in a sling or dog buggy instead, so he can become accustomed to the outside world. It's also light relief for you, as the first few weeks of puppydom can make you feel like a prisoner in your own home.

I used to give my dogs three walks a day, though some days varied. Before breakfast for about 40 minutes, around midday for about an hour (even if it was just pottering around the shops) and before supper for about half an hour. Between walks they are mostly curled up on their beds peacefully, whether I'm there or not, because all their needs have been met. More recently, I have been walking Willa less, as she is too old. But she and my newly acquired puppy are happy with a couple of short walks a day. If, like me, you have dogs of a very different age, or dogs who have different needs for whatever reason, do give them some walks separately. It will give them a chance to walk at their own pace, and give you an opportunity for some one-on-one bonding.

Try and vary the walks. Some on lead, some off lead. Don't always walk the same route. That can get boring. Keep it interesting and exciting. That way you will be draining more energy. Go for a run, bike, scoot or rollerblade with your dog. Walk with different people and different dogs. Open up a world of experiences for him, and ensure they are pleasant experiences. Even a trip to the post office is a walk, so take him with you on errands. Take him on a bus, on a boat, on a train. Although you might not always be walking, it's still a journey, and he'll be using his nose, eyes and ears. It goes without saying that if your dog is reactive to anything outside his safe home, then try and avoid those triggers.

Most importantly let your dog sniff, allowing him to be stimulated and fulfil his natural instincts. Encourage your dog to check in with you every so often, by making eye contact. This reminds him you are walking as a team. It is not advisable to let him fly solo for an entire walk. You want that connection in and out of the house. If you have taken my previous advice, you will have ensured that you are the most interesting thing out there, and the centre of his world.

If you are struggling to give your dog the exercise and fulfilment he needs, hire a dog walker or put him in daycare. But do your homework first. You want someone who is going to echo your ideas about exercise, discipline and affection. Accompany the dog walker on a one of his/her walks before deciding on one. Assess the dynamic of the all the dogs in his/her care. Although the walker can't be expected to manage your dog's behavioural issues, as they'll most likely have a whole pack to attend to, they should be demonstrating some calm control over the dogs, and the dogs should be happy to see them. I'm not so keen on daycare, reason being, there is little direction and often dogs just run around all day getting overstimulated and doing their own thing. Of course they are exhausted when they get home, but what have they learnt? To be bullies, to be fearful? You may be doing more harm than good. Much better to have them trotting behind a walker who is constantly moving and giving direction. That is more in tune with a dog's natural follower state.

Finally, if you just can't get out of bed, and it's raining, and it's the dog walker's day off, then make sure you give your dog more mental stimulation in place of a walk. (Ideas in the previous chapter.) In the absence of being walked or stimulated mentally you may find behavioural issues creeping in, such as destructiveness, barking or howling, hyperactivity, obsessions such as shadow or light chasing, or obsessive licking. The energy has to go somewhere.

CHAPTER 24
Impulse Control

I've devoted a quick chapter to this because I believe it's so important for a dog to be able to stop and think before he acts. If he gets into the habit of looking to his owner before he acts, then he could be avoiding some of his own (often wrong) decisions.

I would like every dog to be able to allow space in his brain for a little thought process before defaulting to his habitual impulsive action. This could mean thinking before automatically lunging or barking at another dog, thinking before automatically chasing that moving thing, thinking before excitedly piling in to play with a dog that might not want to play. If you teach your dog to pause before he acts, you will be able to diffuse many unwanted encounters and situations before they even arise.

Impulse control goes hand in hand with the 'stay' or 'wait' command, which should be practised every day of your dog's life. In a typical day, my dogs will wait and look at me for the signal to follow me through the door for their morning walk. If I have driven to the park, they wait in the back of the car, door open, for the command to get out. No impulsive ricocheting out the minute the boot is raised. In the park, I might throw a ball and ask them to wait before retrieving it. After the walk, they will look at me and wait as I place their breakfast food bowls on the floor and walk away. Only when I give the release command 'OK' can they move forward. And all this controlling of their impulses before the day has barely begun.

I want them to be in the habit of looking to me for direction. If they can trust that I will keep them safe, they should automatically look to me to diffuse the situation, when something uncomfortable arises.

When practising impulse control, the conversation I have with a dog is not a vocal one, like a human would have, but a canine one, using body posture, eye contact and energy. Endless chatter comes across as white noise to a dog. Easy to ignore. Zip it, and see how much more powerful silence is. If you learn to talk dog you will achieve great results.

Let me give you an example. The following method can be used when teaching a dog a 'stay' in any situation. You can use it to teach him to stay back while you open the front door; stay in one room while you go into another; stay at the bottom of the stairs; stay while you put down food; stay on the pavement while you cross a busy main road to retrieve a football – yes I have done this, but suggest you don't try it unless 100% certain of success.

Look the dog in the eye, put a hand up in a stop signal and if you like say 'stay', though it's not necessary. Your body language will do the talking. And whatever you do, do not fall into the trap of repeating 'stay, stay, stay'. Back away slowly, standing tall and looking at the dog. By facing the dog, you are still having a conversation that says "I don't want you to move forward yet". If the dog ignores that and does take a step forward, mirror him and take a step forward towards him. In 90% of cases, he will automatically back up. As soon as he backs up, stop advancing, and back off again. Your retreat tells him he has done the right thing, and you no longer need to 'confront' him. Repeat as many times as you have to until he gets it and stays put. If he finds it too irresistible not to follow you, then make it easier – just back up one step, only make him wait a couple of seconds, then reward. Gradually build on the distance you put between you, and the length of time you make him stay.

There are plenty of games you can play which build on helping him to control his impulses. Start easy. Put some treats in your closed hand. Allow your dog to sniff what's inside. He may start to paw at your hand. Do not open it. If he stops sniffing and pawing or backs off, open your hand. If he pauses for long enough, give him one of the treats from your hand. If he approaches the hand again, close it. This is all done with no words. He is learning that the hand will open and he will be rewarded if he backs off and gives you space. His choices are creating the outcome. It's a great little mental workout too.

Next level up – pop a treat on his paw whilst he is in a lying down position. Start by covering it with your hand. Treat him with the other hand for not going for the treat on his paw. Once he's got the hang of it, you can remove your hand covering the treat, but still reward with the other hand for ignoring the treat on his paw. Now introduce the command 'leave it', as you place the treat on his paw, and reward with the other hand. Build to getting him to give you eye contact before you treat him.

Another challenging one – see if you can get him to walk past a treat or toy and ignore it. Start with him on a lead. You may have to lure his head away from the ground with the smell of a higher value treat under his nose. If he tries to go for what's on the floor, just give a short tug on the lead. Reward with the higher value treat or toy, once he has successfully walked past and ignored the item on the floor. Repeat the above, and introduce the 'leave it' command as you walk past the item on the floor. He should now know what this means. Then reward. This is a useful one for stopping him hoovering up discarded takeaway boxes off the pavement – a downside of life as a Londoner, living a few hundred yards away from a KFC. Eventually, as soon as you say 'leave it', he should then be in the habit of immediately looking up at you to receive his reward, which after lots of practise could come in the form of praise instead of treats.

Dogs that have learnt the ability to manage their own impulses are heads above the rest when it comes to getting themselves out of trouble. Even if their owner is not in close proximity to be able to look towards for help or approval, the dog can still pause, think and make a choice. Even in play, things can escalate pretty quickly to over arousal, which can lead to aggression. After all, chase is part of the hard-wired predatory sequence, and once triggered, it can be hard to switch off. To keep chase safe and fun, a dog needs to be a master of self-control. He might give a mini pause, divert his attention onto something else, sniff the ground or turn his head away, to prevent arousal from escalating. It's very worthwhile teaching your dog the valuable tool of impulse control.

Keeping on the Right Path

My colleague teaching calm and control to Scout,
with the help of her spaniels.

Willa staying beautifully one side of the road,
with me the other side, as a car passes.

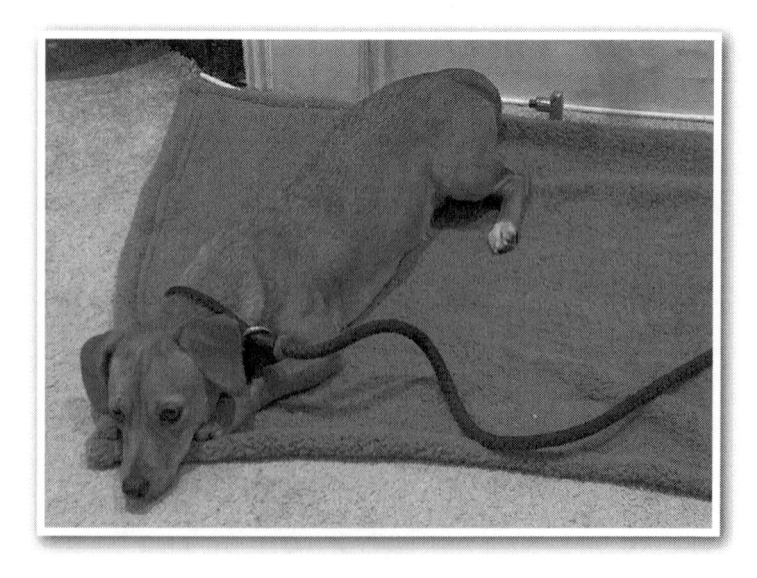

Teaching a client's dog to stay on his bed. He's doing it,
but he hasn't gone into relaxation yet. See the furrowed brow
and pricked ears, and back legs ready to spring forward.

CHAPTER 25
Communication

Our dogs have adapted admirably to a life of domesticity. They spend much of their time watching us, and can read our facial expression, mood and routine. They know when we are going on holiday by the frisson of excitement and the packed bags in the hall. They know when they are going for a walk the second you pick up your keys or put on your coat. They have literally learnt to understand our language. Before she went deaf, my Labrador knew the difference between 'get the stick' and 'get the ball'. My other dog knows at least 15 words. Many dogs know more. So, with dogs adapting to us so willingly, do we not owe it to them to learn a bit of their language? To read their body posture, their facial expression; to differentiate between an insecure bark and a confident bark. To talk dog. Communication is, after all, a two-way thing. If we are to create a harmonious and loving bond between animal and human, then trust and understanding are paramount.

I have read countless books, poured over multiple video clips and endless real life interactions, and attended multiple seminars, in my quest to further understand the fascinating and often very subtle language of dogs. I won't bore you with minute detail here, but I would like to dispel a few myths, and point out 'green flag' (acceptable) and 'red flag' (warning) body language and behaviour, so you can step in where necessary and save your dog some stress.

Firstly, the myths:

1. *Dogs look guilty and know when they have done wrong.*

   You know the look – head lowered, eyes raised, showing the whites of their eyes (whale eye). No. Dogs do not experience guilt. They are living in the present moment and are merely reacting with appeasement to your expression which looks threatening.

2. *Raised hackles means the dog is feeling anger or aggression.*

   No. It just shows that the dog is unsure. It is an involuntary reflex, caused by adrenaline pushing up the muscles, called piloerection, triggered when the dog is in a state of arousal, excitement or even anxiety. The human phrase is misleading. If someone raises my hackles, they annoy or anger me. Not so in the dog world.

3. *A wagging tail means the dog is happy.*

   It can do. But it can also mean the dog is over stimulated, aroused, unsure or excited. The tail wag must be read in accordance with the dog's other body language. For example, a tail held high and wagging very quickly, with a stiff body and high head, ears pricked, signals the dog is overstimulated. He is disseminating his scent vigorously and uncovering his anal gland to the full. Dogs have bitten in this state of mind. A tail held midway, parallel to the ground and gently wagging, with a soft and fluid body, head held midway without ears pricked, signals a friendly dog who is pleased to meet you. A tail held between the legs wagging quickly is trying to cover the scent from the anal gland. Head and body are usually low and ears back in this scenario. The dog is insecure and does not want to give his scent away. The wagging is a nervousness, and may be accompanied by rolling onto his back in appeasement.

4. *A yawning dog means he is tired.*
   Not always. It can also mean he is stressed. The yawn allows the dog to breathe in more oxygen, in preparation for fight or flight.

5. *Dogs are capable of doing protest poos.*
   Not true. Dogs do not hold grudges, or plan what they will do in the future. They live in the present moment. If your dog has soiled the house, it is more likely because he has been left on his own for longer than he can cope with, and he is stressed, or literally can't hold it in.

6. *Rolling over is a submissive gesture.*
   It can be. But it's all about the context. When a dog rolls over he is exposing his genitals (and his scent) and the most vulnerable part of his body, and effectively saying "Look I'm no threat". But in some 'play' circumstances he rolls onto his back to push the other dog (or human) away with his paws. He is saying, "Get away from me".

7. *A play bow is an invitation to play.*
   It can be. But again, we need to look at the context. Sarah Whitehead, author of 'Clever Dog' noticed that in 80% of incidences when a dog initiated a play bow, play did not ensue. Moreover, it made the other dog flee. Her deduction was that play bows are used to make the other dog (or person) move away. In some cases, this was so the 'bower' could engage in chase, in others it was just because the 'bower' wanted some space.

8. *"He's only playing."*
   How many times have you heard this from the owner of a dog who is harassing yours? Chances are, if it doesn't feel right to you, it's not right. I have included this in the myth section because so often other owners falsely believe that their dog's intentions are good, when they are anything but. No-one knows your dog better than you, and if he looks uncomfortable or comes to hide between your legs, listen to him, he's trying to communicate with you, so take him out of there.

Play and chase should be balanced, and one dog should not be permitted to bully another. If it's your dog doing the bullying, take him away. You don't want him learning that this is acceptable behaviour.

Bullying behaviour includes putting paws or chin on another dog's neck, targeted bites, chasing without letting the other dog take a turn in chasing, harassment when the other dog clearly isn't interested, mounting. Remember context is key – some of these behaviours are used in play quite benignly. Don't assume that just because your dog is being mounted by another dog that it is bullying. What is your dog's other body language telling you? If he's giving as much as he gets, then it's probably fine, but if his body and head are lowered, tail between the legs, ears back and trying to move away, then he's clearly not enjoying it.

Green Flag (benign) Behaviour:

- Soft eyes.
- Relaxed facial muscles.
- Soft, wiggly body.
- Lowering of body and head – says "Look how small I am, I'm no threat".
- Open mouth, soft tongue.
- Tail held midway.
- Gentle tail-wagging.
- Ears back so you can see the insides of them.

- Non-direct approaches – may approach in an arc, or with pauses, and presents their body side on.
- Head turn – politely saying "I'm not interested in you", avoids eye contact.
- Mirroring and matching another dog in movement and play.
- Self-handicapping – a bigger dog may lie down to play with a smaller dog, or a faster dog may slow down so the other can catch him.
- Pausing – on greeting or during play (different from a body freeze).
- Body shake – shaking off a (usually tense) state of mind.
- Stalking.
- Looking to humans.

Red Flag (warning) Behaviour:

- Hard eyes.
- Tense facial muscles and frowning.
- Closed, tense mouth with lips pulled back.
- Lip curl.
- Head held high, ears pricked.
- Tail held high, intense, quick wagging.
- Intense stare and direct approach in straight line.
- Freeze, when body is motionless; precedes fight or flight.
- Whale eye – when you can see the whites of the eyes; indicates uncertainty.

- Laying paws or chin on another dog's neck.
- Body blocking – when a dog controls the direction of movement of another dog.
- Mounting.
- Hackles up (signifies unsure).
- Nose jab.
- Revealing teeth – look at my weapons, keep back.
- Growling, barking, lunging.

Stress signals:

- Panting (when not hot).
- Lip licking, tongue flicks – the wetness of a dog's nose means it can hold odour molecules; the tongue gathers information from it in the form of scent.
- Sweaty paws.
- Yawning (when not tired) – the body is taking in more oxygen in readiness for fight or flight.
- Tail tucked between the legs.
- Shedding (keep this in context – obviously not every dog that sheds is stressed).
- Pacing.
- Whining.
- Destructive behaviour.
- Chewing their own limbs.
- Inappropriate toileting (when house trained).
- Dilated pupils.
- Extended tongue.
- Tail-chasing and other obsessive behaviours such as carpet-licking.

- Rapid blinking – as any form of fixed stare would seem like a direct challenge.
- Bulging eyes.
- Whale eye – when head moves away but eyes stay on you, revealing the whites of the eyes. (I'm always reminded of the classic Princess Diana coy pose.)
- Ears pinned flat back against the head.
- Shaking and trembling – release of adrenaline in preparation for fight or flight.
- Hunched body.
- Moving in slow motion.
- Excessive barking.

Whale eye.

Keeping on the Right Path

The better you can understand your dog's body language, the better the communication, and hence relationship, between the two of you. It is also worth noting how your dog may be translating your body language. Here are a few classic examples of miscommunication:

Scenario 1

You see an old man with a walking stick coming towards you, so you automatically pull back on the lead to give him room to pass.

You think: I'm teaching my dog to give passers-by respectful space.

Your dog thinks: my human obviously feels threatened by this on-coming man, as he has gone all tense, so I'd better protect us by barking and lunging to make the threat go away, because I can't flee, which I'd rather do, as I'm on the lead.

Your dog has learnt to bark at men with walking sticks.

Scenario 2

You return home to find your dog has defecated in the kitchen. (Probably through stress of being left on his own for too long, I might add.) You scold him, and put his face near the poo to show him what you are cross about.

You think: I'm teaching him that pooing in the house is unacceptable.

Your dog thinks: when my owner comes home, he will be intimidating, even though I show him I am no threat. Oh, and he has a weird fixation about poo.

Your dog has learnt to hide or cower from you when you enter the room, and to only poo where you can't find it – in the corner of the top bedroom maybe. Or perhaps he will eat it so you can't find it at all.

Scenario 3
You are about to have a baby, so you think it's a good idea to get the dog used to having his toys and food removed, in case the toddler gets between him and his stuff. While your dog is mid-meal, you pick up his bowl and put it down again several times.

You think: I'm teaching my dog not to guard his food.

Your dog thinks: this is intensely annoying. If he keeps doing that, I will growl to show him my displeasure, and if he ignores my growl, I'll go straight for the bite next time.

Your dog has learnt to resource guard his possessions and become aggressive around food.

Scenario 4
You are walking in the countryside and your dog gives chase to a deer. You sternly shout his name repeatedly until he eventually returns. You yell 'bad dog' at him and maybe even give him a whack.

You think: he'll never chase a deer again after this telling off.

Your dog thinks: my owner is very cross about something, I better keep away from him.

Your dog has learnt not to return to you next time you shout his name.

Scenario 5
You are teaching your dog to stay, so you repeat 'stay, stay, stay' as you back away.

You think: as long as I repeat the command, he will continue to stay.

Your dog thinks: he wants me to stay, so I will stay. Oh no, I must be doing something wrong as he keeps asking me to do this thing, which I'm obviously not getting right, so I'll try moving forward instead and see if that works.

Your dog has learnt, well, nothing! He's rather confused.

In all the scenarios it is important to understand that it's not the dog who has been badly behaved. Ironically, it is the owner who has taught the dog the 'bad' behaviour. The dog is just falling into line.

Afterword

Our dogs' behaviour is our creation, consciously or unconsciously. Dogs are not born bad. I have never met a bad dog. Many bad owners, but no bad dogs.

Knowledge is power, and once my clients have the knowledge, they get the very best out of their dogs. They can comprehend that their dog behaves as he does due to the circumstances forced upon him, rather than through any choice of his own.

Next time you get angry with your dog for being naughty, stop and ask yourself, "What have I done to create this behaviour?" I hope the penny will drop, you will change your behaviour, for it is you I am training, not the dog, and you will conclude with the words, "Good dog".

I cannot ever perceive living without a dog. I am very blessed to be able to make my passion my work. It is an incredibly rewarding job. We have so much to learn from these gracious creatures. They are second to none at reading our mood, and supporting us, no matter what.

I believe the world would be a better place if we were able to 'be more dog' and love unconditionally, accept the things we cannot change, play without needing to win, show not hide your feelings, not judge someone by their age, race or looks, learn the art of doing nothing at all, be less critical, be more spontaneous, be more open minded, be more forgiving and know that every day is the best day.

Excerpt taken from "Be More Dog"
by Fenella Nicholas

I would love to hear from any readers with their own particular stories. Or if it's help you need, I'll do my best to support you. Do get in touch via the contact form of my website www.bemoredog.guru.

Notes

NO SUCH THING AS A BAD DOG

Notes

NO SUCH THING AS A BAD DOG